Necessary Steps

Necessary Steps

poetry • elegy • walking • spirit

edited by

David Kennedy

Shearsman Books
Exeter

Published in the United Kingdom in 2007 by
Shearsman Books Ltd
58 Velwell Road
Exeter EX4 4LD

ISBN-13   978-1-905700-63-9

ISBN-10   1-905700-63-6

Acknowledgements
The essays by Andrea Brady, John Hall, Peter Middleton, Jennifer Moxley, Malcolm
Phillips and Michael Symmons Roberts, and the interview with Stuart Mugridge
were originally published in *The Paper*. They are reprinted here by permission of
the authors. All but the first of Peter Riley's 'Walking Pieces' previously appeared
in the author's *The Day's Final Balance. Uncollected Writings 1965-2006* (Shearsman
Books, 2007) and are reproduced here by permission of the author.

In Penelope Shuttle's 'The Whole World's Water', we are grateful to The Rialto
for permission to quote 'The Rose Takes Over' by Julia Casterton, from *The Doves
of Finisterre*, copyright © 2004, Julia Casterton; and to Jonathan Clowes Ltd, on
behalf of Julia Watson, for 'Rest' by Alan Curtis, copyright © 2004, Alan Curtis.

The publisher gratefully acknowledges
the financial assistance of Arts Council England.

Contents

Introduction

The starting point for this book was a desire to bring to a wider readership some of the critical and reflective prose that originally appeared in *The Paper*, the magazine of poetry and poetics that I edited and published from 2001 to 2004. After re-reading some twenty or so contributions, it became apparent that the richest ones—six essays and one interview—dealt with one of three subjects: elegy, walking or the spiritual. The richness of all seven pieces derives from their authors' consciousness of changes in the late modern period to the cultural, political, psychological and social structures that govern not only—to borrow Denise Riley's memorable formulation—'the words of selves' but also the responsibilities of words and selves to others.

I am not talking about post-modernism here since that notorious 'post' only functions negatively to articulate, say, a failure of political consciousness or an unwillingness to expend the effort necessary to work through the implications of modernism. My seven original authors, it seems to me, are doing something much more interesting and urgent. They are all engaging, in their very different ways, with the fact that, although structures change, what Peter Middleton calls in the context of contemporary elegy 'existential difficulty' continues to manifest itself in 'emotions, memories, biographical questions, and metaphysical speculations, whose turbulence can overwhelm interpretive clarity and yet whose relevance cannot be dismissed'. So, for example, Malcolm Phillips sees in Apollinaire's walks across Paris and Frank O'Hara's strolls around Manhattan 'anxieties about desire and death' which continue to circulate in both individual lives and national narratives. Michael Symmons Roberts reads David Jones's story of walking to find the source of a stopped stream in 1917 as a still resonant image of an unacknowledged and unfashionable need for spiritual sustenance.

It is such questions and speculations, then, that provide the kernel of what follows and to which other invited contributions have been added. There is no single theme to this book. In what follows, instead of giving a summary of each contribution, I shall try to give a sense of the many questions that circulate within the book and around its subtitle 'poetry · elegy · walking · spirit'.

★ ★ ★ ★ ★

In a brief introduction to the poetry of Carol Mirakove, Keston Sutherland reminds us that a classic account of self-possession occurs towards the end of Book IV of *The Prelude*. Wordsworth recounts how 'a favourite pleasure' is to walk at night along the deserted 'public Way'. On one such occasion, he 'slowly mounted up a steep ascent' and gained at last a hallucinatory solitude which brought 'A self-possession felt in every pause / And gentle movement of my frame.' Sutherland observes that it's no longer possible for us to walk away and stand aside: 'there's no ascent so steep that you won't find part of a junk-food chain at its mighty crest.' Nonetheless, Sutherland goes on, Wordsworth 'laid out as *realities* the conditions for self-possession that we now recognize as *cancelled possibilities*. This was a terrific achievement.'

Wordsworth's 'terrific achievement' in Book IV of *The Prelude*—and in other famous passages like the episode of the stolen boat in Book I—was also to establish poetry itself as the space of solitary self-possession. This is perhaps one meaning of the ending of Frank O'Hara's 'A Step Away from Them': 'My heart is in my / pocket, it is Poems by Pierre Reverdy.' After a walk through the midday bustle of New York and all its distractions—including the poet's own desires stirred up by what he sees—it is poetry that allows him to collect and recollect himself. He regains his self-possession. The closing lines somehow reconfigure and restore the poem as a moment of private silence.

'A Step Away from Them', written the day after Jackson Pollock's funeral, is a species of elegy not only for Pollock but also for O'Hara's close friends Bunny Lang and John Latouche. The regaining of self-possession is crucial to elegy and Wordsworth's scene of self-possession converges with the classic scene of English pastoral elegy. The speaker of a poem like, say, Milton's 'Lycidas' or Matthew Arnold's 'Thyrsis' also walks alone at night or as night falls in order to grieve and finally collect or re-collect his thoughts and find consolation. The elegist's restlessness is a way of allowing the dead to walk the earth one final time before finding peace. The elegist is simultaneously mourner, revenant and exorcist.

Further insight into self-possession and into the work of mourning are given by the final episode of Book IV of *The Prelude* in which the poet meets a discharged soldier. The soldier is propped against a milestone, 'half-sitting, and half-standing', rooted to the spot and uttering sounds 'as if of pain / Or of uneasy thought' in 'a murmuring voice of dead complaint'. Wordsworth hails him and the man tells his tale with a manner that is 'unmov'd' and in a voice of 'mild indifference'. The soldier's demeanour seems to prefigure Freud's classic account of the melancholic. In contrast to Wordsworth, he is unable to restore his 'listless sense' and 'exhausted mind' by walking in order to rediscover 'some distant region of [the] soul'. In common parlance, he is unable to 'move on'.

The walking poem that repositions the self in the universe and the elegy that puts the dead in their proper place underline connections between walking, poetry and the spiritual. One might recall here the pilgrims who walk to Compostela; Seamus Heaney walking with the dead in *Station Island*; and Les Murray's remark that all religions are 'large poems'. Murray's view converges with M. H. Abrams's observation that the Victorian period's strict binary of imaginative vs. rational meant that 'religion ... was converted into poetry, and poetry into a kind of religion.' The so-called mainstream poem—that store cupboard curry of confession, diary and observation—still performs this function. For example, Michael Hofmann's 'In Connemara' ends 'on the panting hills, where the wind / tightens its cries and blows them away' and typifies the way such poems seem to apprehend the ineffable in the exact moment of saying it can never be apprehended or possessed. Loss, we might say, becomes our version of the spiritual. Cancelled possibilities are reconfigured as pleasure and lost self-possession is celebrated in the uneasy manner of a retirement party. The so-called avant-garde or experimental poem responds to cancellation and loss with a sense of hurt that can turn to anger. Its response is to attempt to return the language of the poem and thereby the writing and reading self to something approaching full—or at least fuller—consciousness. Deprived of self-possession, it tries to repossess language.

The connections sketched in the preceding paragraphs—between solitude, self-possession, walking, poetry, mourning, the spiritual—are also some of the paths explored by the writers in this book. The essays are arranged simply in alphabetical order to allow them to step on each other's toes and to invite the reader to venture off the beaten track. It is a happy accident but perhaps not surprising that the book starts and finishes with essays on how to write about loss in an age of lost forms.

To return to O'Hara's poem, the peculiarity of its famous question—'But is the / earth as full as life was full, of them?'—derives in large part from the fact that such a question can barely be articulated in the urban spaces of capitalist desire which are '12:40 of / a Thursday'. In contrast to the pastoral scene of elegy, there is nothing animal or vegetable in Manhattan which will answer 'yes' by bowing down a pensive head or weeping with the poet.

A common thread running through many of the pieces gathered here, then, is what consciousness of cancelled possibilities does to one's sense of form. It is not only questions about death that are harder and harder to frame. It may be that the walk and the poem give us a sense—however temporary, however illusory—of cancelled possibilities being reopened.

David Kennedy
Sheffield 2007

Works Cited

M. H. Abrams, *The Mirror and The Lamp: Romantic Theory and the Critical Tradition* (Oxford: OUP, 1971) p.335.

Michael Hofmann, *Nights in the Iron Hotel* (London: Faber and Faber, 1983), p.18.

Frank O'Hara, *Selected Poems* (Manchester: Carcanet, 1991), p.110–111: p.111.

Les Murray, *The Paperbark Tree: Selected Prose* (London: Minerva, 1993), p.252.

Keston Sutherland, 'For Carol Mirakove', in *"the darkness surrounds us": American Poetry*, edited by Sam Ladkin and Robin Purves, published as *Edinburgh Review* 114, pp.186–190: p.187.

William Wordsworth, *The Prelude*, 1805 text (Oxford: OUP, 1986), respectively, ll.363–399 and ll.400–449, pp.63–5.

Now is the Night:
Notes on Kevin Nolan's Elegiac Doubles

ANDREA BRADY

I. Some Contexts for Thinking about *Alar*

Is the soul a sailor or a musician? These analogies help to organize a range of references in Kevin Nolan's first published chapbook, *Alar* (Cambridge: Equipage, 1997). In *De Anima* (II.i, 413a), Aristotle confesses that 'it remains unclear whether the soul is the actuality of a body in this way or rather is as the sailor of a boat,' a comparison which has been attributed to Plato. Three kinds of sailors are relevant to this text: Ulysses (a.k.a. Enlightenment reason); the navigator who crosses the meridians, lines marking the 'middle of the day'; and the soul steering the body towards death. Referencing the first of these in its title, J. H. Prynne's poem 'Lashed to the Mast' from *The White Stones*, a volume whose influence on *Alar* (in particular its language of music, patience, name and number) could be the subject of another essay, addresses a 'you' who has 'everything', 'rising now / in the east', from 'aboard our dauncing boat'.[1] Nolan's elegy for the philosopher Gillian Rose, 'Patience in the Mines', wants 'your declension' to 'relive, *to hear sounds of love in the thunderstorm*'; Prynne's poem warns its recipient to watch the thunder. Prynne offers as imperative or observation: 'love the / forgetfulness of man which is / our prime notion of praise'. It stakes out the necessity of poetic commemoration in man's lovable feebleness, his forgetfulness. But the needful things—the need to memorialise—are 'sacral / convergence' that 'grove on / a hill we know too much of', i.e. Parnassus, the haunt of the muses. Instead, 'this with no name & place / is us'. We, 'you, I', are identified and in a sense collectivized by the disappearance of our name and place into demonstrative 'this'-ness. We pace the Parnassian grove, offering praise in a futile effort to forestall the 'forgetfulness of man'. This forgetting of name and place is also to be loved, as part of the holy sequence of existence and disappearance.

Alar can be read as an elegiac sequence into which Nolan inscribes 'Patience in the Mines' by linking its title to the last line of the preceding poem 'An Abhainn Dubh': 'each time you listen, patience the name itself'. This coronal link between the two texts is also indicative of the importance of the concept of 'patience' in *Alar*, another characteristic it shares with Prynne's *The White Stones*. As Keston Sutherland explains it, 'Prynne suggests that philology can be radicalised by *patience*: that is, by sufferance of its present incapacities, which are really the distance of the experience of discourse in history from our present experience of it.' He offers the etymology of 'patience' from the Latin *patientia*, suffering. Early uses of the word signal that 'Patience is a means of self-possession.' Sutherland continues: the 'nexus of *patience—possession—immanence*, central to Prynne's work of the 1960s, is at once an etymological and an ontological nexus, originating both in the past (the history of language now occluded by changes in meaning and usage) and in the future into which Prynne "waits" for it to re-emerge.'[2] 'Patience in the Mines' pays tribute to that experience of self-possession ('mines') in suffering, to the forms of knowledge that emerged in particular from Gillian Rose's experience of physical pain and more generally from an openness to mourning.

Like *The White Stones*, *Alar* frequently turns from suffering to the consolations and continuities of music, while admitting the futility of singing '*why war* now war is over'. Music also provides us with a second analogy for the soul. Coleridge described the soul as 'a being inhabiting our body and playing upon it, like a musician enclosed in an organ whose keys were placed inwards' (*Letters*, i.278). The momentarily Whitman-like speaker of *Alar* proclaims 'I sing my has-been brothers and sisters'. This livid book is full of carols and dirges. In 'Events Near Bantry' 'everything is singing': the fallen are 'picked up' to riot again, while the 'less vertical creatures' act as 'pall-bearers in a / New Year Dance band'. This is a jovial Irish wake, resounding with 'frosty sax' at midnight. The soul musician plays the body's organ, ranging through the 'diapason quite by itself' ('Baion with Soft Metal to Come'). Diapason is the octave, that simple golden interval formed of a 2:1 ratio between frequencies, by a doubling of tones. The figure of the double, in person and language, will emerge as an important theme in this book. The *baion* is a Brazilian beat, and we can read 'soft metal' as a musical genre; but in the oncoming phrase 'no / pyrrhic lesion but clamour of soft metals to choose / and end', the soft metal implements are clamoring to be used, to bring about that chosen end which guarantees the Stoic's ultimate freedom. The suicidal option darkens the living shores of these elegies:

'my wrists / crane for past life by the station', aching to make life a thing of the past, Nolan writes in 'Patience in the Mines'.

But these lines could also be read as a phenomenological ascription of knowledge to the body itself: even my wrists ache for the past. In this and other ways, *Alar* could be considered a polemical response to Wittgenstein's theory of the soul as a linguistic expression of interiority rather than as Aristotelian *eidos*, or as 'the psychological and spiritual entity pervaded by the city and the sacred' which is part of Gillian Rose's triune broken middle.[3] [Wittgenstein postulates paradoxically that 'death is not an event in life', 'the world and life are one', and 'the world is *my* world: this is manifest in the fact that the limits of *language* (of that language which alone I understand) mean the limits of *my* world'.[4] For Wittgenstein, the 'soul' is rhetorical figure by which we communicate our experience of pain, grief or hope.] Language is exterior to the object world with which we identify it: 'Thought, language, now appear to us as the unique correlate, picture, of the world', equivalent to the world, but not identical with it.[5] Unlike Aristotle, who attributes a soul to all living objects which move or have perception, Wittgenstein declares that the stone and the dog cannot have a soul: 'Only of what behaves like a human being can one say that it has pains'. The stone has no sensation; the wriggling fly or the dog can feel pain, but cannot communicate their experiences by the language games of the ensouled. We can only share the pain of other subjects through idealist concepts which reside in the mind rather than in the afflicted body.

Nolan recognises the broad challenges these arguments pose to the elegist, striving to accommodate the departed soul in language, by quoting Wittgenstein (*Philosophical Investigations* §357) in 'Events Near Bantry': 'If one sees the behaviour of a living thing, one sees its soul'. In that poem, the philosopher is described as an actuary of the material body, 'the manager of clay with the / brindled accent'. He may also be present in the elegy 'Au Hasard Godfrey Cambridge', where the ferry comes 'in a white halation playing back its chains' of memory. Wittgenstein wrote (*Philosophical Investigations* §97) that 'Thought is surrounded by a halo': although it is required to be 'of the purest crystal', an idealization which banishes 'empirical cloudiness or uncertainty'. As Nolan writes, 'you knead your / hat and think that money and change are crystals', reifications of material relations, abstractions which have become as transparent as crystal. The 'ich-crystal finish' ('Seven Last Words') reflects the hardening of the concept of the 'I' but also the inconceivability of its finitude in death. Crystals make another appearance in the text. In 'An Abhainn Dubh', Nolan refers to John Tyndall, the Irish naturalist who published an influential treatise on crystals in 1848. Tyndall was also famous for his observation that without water vapour the earth's surface would be 'held fast in the iron grip of frost'. The original version of 'Patience in the Mines' declares that 'Frost grips the stone observatory', changed to 'cadmium vapour' in *Alar*. This 'frost' provokes Coleridgean associations: the friends 'list at midnight by Greenwich stairs', a line which is deleted in the *Alar* version of the poem, or who 'count the stars this midnight' rather than 'mean-/time' in *Alar*. But the book retains references to iron and crystal elsewhere: iron filings in a ricerar (another musical form), 'earth-marked iron', 'ice-/crystals under her collar', 'where gold and / iron were rent'. In this iron age of industrial production, the desire for love must be encircled 'with bands of iron', according to Prynne's poem 'Song in Sight of the World'. Metaphorically, the grounds of human activity can be relaxed by the precipitation of mourning, which *Alar*'s version of 'Patience in the Mines' allows to fall as 'a double rain' over London. This double elegiac rain is both real and sentimental, precipitation and tears, mourning for the dead other and for the self.

This doubling—of the places of the living and the dead—is part of a larger double action in *Alar*, which reflects the importance of doubles and chiasmus to Rose's philosophy as well. Of the dead, Nolan remarks 'How the whiteness claims them, hunger for likeness'. They are claimed by that blanked-out space of whiteness which throughout the book signals death, as well as disease and physical corruption. The phrase 'hunger for likeness' derives from *The Culture of the Copy* by Hillel Schwartz, a book which investigates the profound desire for, and construction of legends around, a dead or missing twin or double. Gillian Rose writes about the double identities of authors such as Kierkegaard, Arendt and Luxemburg. She describes their self-exposure to "double danger" as an exploration within the agon of authorship of 'what it is to succumb either to worldly or to otherworldly authority'. It 'is the *only undangerous position*: the only one, literally, that does not liberate from one dominion—for 'danger' comes etymologically from Latin, *dominus*, 'lord'—to submit to another. Anxiety of beginning and equivocation of the middle—restlessness that yet remains with both dangers—is the only way to avoid the spiritual, social and political inversions which attend any alleviation'.[6] The marks of double danger are *aporia* (the difficulty of relation between the singular and the universal) and *agape* (p. 165). Rose consistently rejects the post-modernist view which would redeem the Other, the unidentical twin of the self or reason, from subjugation by exiling reason. In a later work, Rose describes the double danger of lovemaking as an ethical encounter with the Other. She writes that 'To spend the whole night with someone is *agape*: it is ethical. For you must move with him and with yourself from the arms of the one twin to the abyss of the other', from eros to the passion of faith.[7] This joint navigation onto the dangerous shores of waking 'brings you into the shared cares of the finite world'. In this essay, I will read Nolan's elegy for Rose, 'Patience in the Mines', as the journey of a surviving twin through the night.

II. Twins and Double-Crossings

The title of *Alar* plays both on the wings (Latin, *ala, -ae*, f.) on which time's chariot hurries near, the wing-shaped structures of the body (as in the nostrils), and the chemical daminozide which controls the colour and decay rate of apples—the fruit which first brought death to man. That alar or daminozide causes cancer is, of course, grimly relevant to a book which includes poems commemorating two people who died of the disease—Henrietta Lacks and Gillian Rose. Lacks was an African-American woman who died of cervical cancer in 1951 and whose cells have been cultured in labs around the world, used to test everything from cosmetics to the effects of the atom bomb. Her cells 'were so prolific that there is more of her now, in terms of biomass, than there ever was when she was alive'—and they were the first to live beyond the 50th generation. Another elegy, for the lawyer Roy Cohn (an assistant to Joseph McCarthy), watches as 'life drowns life in the flux of immutable love, each day with its compass of malic lesions, IVU'. Cohn died of AIDS in 1986; the 'malic lesions' are probably Kaposi's sarcoma. But malic acid is a fruit acid. In this invocation of Donne's 'Valediction Forbidding Mourning', Nolan describes the lesions of mortality rather than eros and justice as providing the metaphysical compass for the orientation of mourning.

Nolan's elegy for Rose, who died on 9 December 1995, was originally published as a photocopied broadside, and some revisions were made to the text before its republication in *Alar* in 1997. The broadside is backed by an image of anti-aircraft fire tracing fine white lines and bursting in small star-like flames above a silhouetted city. This city is probably Sarajevo, besieged by Serbian forces between April 1992 and February 1996. That war ended in 1995, which would account for the revision of this text when it was republished in 1997 to read 'now war is over' rather than 'when war is over'. The title of the Rose elegy is probably a reference to Samuel Johnson's famous elegy 'On the Death of Mr. Robert Levet', a doctor whose ministrations to his patients could not protect him from his own death. That poem opens: 'Condemn'd to Hope's delusive mine, / As on we toil from day to day...' Medicine can prop up its patients with delusive hopes of recovery; perhaps Nolan is suggesting that the philosopher treats herself to similar metaphysical palliations. While her late books *Love's Work* and *Paradiso* offer no consolation about the savagery of cancer's assault on her guts and her life, they also chronicle her turn towards Christian faith. The Scriptures (John 8:7) are quoted at least once in 'Patience in the Mines': 'you in mourning cast, first stone of spring!' In the *Alar* version of the poem, Nolan writes: 'Spare me the patience of your ruin, to / decussate a language thick with music'. (This amends the line 'spare me the patience of your hatred / in a language thick with music' in the earlier version of the poem.) In this ambivalent imperative, the elegist is asking for the benediction of patience, and complaining that he refuses to accept Rose's patient, stoical composure in the ruins of her life. Decussated language is scored or crossed with the shape of an X or a T: the shape of a surgical incision, of the figure of chiasmus, and of the crucifix. This incision breaks the flow of the musical phrase, the 'flux of immutable love' ('Seven Last Words'). Our awareness of her death scars our reading of Rose's language; but we must also retain our composure in order to operate critically on her texts.

Crossing and doubling in language are significant topoi throughout *Alar*, an elegiac book concerned with the ethical responsibilities of the poet or survivor who seeks to memorialize the dead through activities in language. Crossing and doubling are invoked in 'Abbiamo Wanstead', where we are

> up to our mouths to make ends meet,
> in paradiastole to this chamfered crush
> *to join the mean with each extremity*
> some middle aim through earth-marked iron,
> the one music, the other contradiction

It is up to our mouths—to our politic or subtle use of language—to force contradictory ends into concurrence. We may also be drowning in the practicalities of making ends meet. Opposing means and ends are both crushed together, and chamfered, their synthesis marked with a groove or cut. Rose would approve of this incomplete reconciliation of opposites, where each bears the mortal scars of their convergence, those 'fissures of still straining contraries' which postmodernism cannot erase (*The Broken Middle* xii). But paradiastole would hide the scars of this reconciliation. A figure of extenuation, paradiastole is a form of flattering rhetoric, which soothes the object of praise by referring to its vices as virtues—the epideictic poet's fingers 'reach for / lull and scorn' ('Slough over Time'). A virtuoso exploration of the political uses of paradiastole is Thomas Wyatt's poem 'Mine own John Poyntz', from which the third line of the above extract is taken. Inviting his friend Poyntz to join him in Kent, Wyatt explains his alienation from court as his inability 'with the nearest virtue to cloak away the vice'. Nolan also eschews the flattery which elegiac decorum usually requires, most significantly in 'The Seven Last Words of Roy Cohn'. He seems to share with Rose a rejection of the mean, a commitment to the pursuit of the extremity. In *Love's Work*, for example, Rose writes of 'the mean of friendship' as a diminished alternative to the passionate love which is her 'life affair'.

This temperamental commitment to the extreme is not the only point of sympathy between the two. They seem also to share in the opposition to post-structuralist theories of language; as Nolan argues in an essay on 'Getting Past Odradek', 'the arbitrary sign replaces the arbitrary body: language becomes the causality of fate'. Against this principle of arbitrary substitution, in 'The Seven Last Words of Roy

Cohn' Nolan observes or wishes 'That the fidelity of thought live in self-suppletion before that which transcends it'. Suppletion is the grammatical term for the replacement of a verb's stem with another, in conjugations such as 'go' and 'went'. For thought to remain faithful to its object, Nolan suggests, it must break through crystallised abstractions and replace its own root with another, higher thesis. Thought will then be scarred with its history, faithful to this dialectical movement and substitution of unlikes as a movement towards completion. Self-suppletion also identifies the presence of the uncanny in the ordinary, of the foreign in the homely. This is another expression of Nolan's demand for 'no *unheimlich* without a primordial self encounter, reckoning at its true cost the amount of *Willkür* left not merely to continue (live on) but to act on'.[8] Similarly, Rose writes that the name of the beloved 'abolishes the safe uncanniness of the ordinary'; in erotic suppletion, you call my name, which 'at every thrust returns me not to myself, but to the root of you flush in me' (*Love's Work* p. 64). This erotic vitality of the absolute uniqueness of the name and the body, both occupied by passion's twin, haunts the memorialisation of the dead who have 'no name & place' anymore.

The connection between doubling or crossing in language and images of scarring and lesions is made clear by the book's second epigraph from the nineteenth century neurologist John Hughlings Jackson: 'to locate the damage which destroys speech, and to locate speech, are two different things'. This remark may be considered as a response to the discoveries of Philippe de Broca, the nineteenth century neuroscientist whose study of aphasia enabled him to localize the brain centre for articulate speech in the third convolution of the left frontal lobe. The premise that the origin of speech can only be discerned once the capacity for speech has been lost is fundamental to elegiac work. It is as if the marks struck into the page themselves originate in loss of the memorialized individuals to the diseases of 'whiteness'. The text struggles to weave back together the raveled threads of dense life, the neural connections 'leucotomized' in an effort to combat depression or grief. It expresses the wish 'to cross from shoreline to shore / frame and fissure what you are' ('Au Hasard'), to return from the black waters, crossing that line of dying which both frames and fractures what *you* are. Etymology reveals the violence required to force the restoration of these connections. Paradiastole signals a rupture or splitting, a violation of truth which moves outward, away from the object's true qualities.

The difference between textual and real scars is also in evidence. A reference to the 'desocupado lector' or idle reader in 'Baion with Soft Metal to Come' alludes to the preface to *Don Quixote*. In the first chapter of that text, the narrator describes the effect of reading books of chivalry on Quixote. Conceits like 'pearls' and passages such as 'the reason of the unreason with which my reason is afflicted so weakens my reason...' perplex him. Similarly, Roy Cohn is 'ready for another line of pearl dust', of cocaine and delusion. Quixote is uneasy about the many wounds suffered by Don Belianis, because 'he must have had his face and body covered all over with seams and scars'. Fictional scars can disappear into narrative, while the real body would have to carry the marks of its suffering. The pain of another body—what for Wittgenstein can only be communicated, not experienced empathetically—is one of the most significant themes in Rose's *Love's Work*, which declares its intention to invent 'colostomy ethnography'. Would it be ghoulish to suggest that her suffering body *itself* became the broken middle? Rose's work does return again and again to the analogies between the soul, the city and the sacred. Perhaps her somatic scars stand for the pain of *aporia* as she describes it:

> Edna tells me that the 'tranquil use' of *aporia*, in the classical Greek philosophy of Plato and in Aristotle, means literally 'no passage', hence philosophical difficulty or lack of resolution; it has a biblical equivalent of an altogether more drastic tone. In the Septuagint, the Greek translation of the Hebrew Scriptures, *aporia*, translates *behalah*, which means, 'dismay, sudden terror, or ruin'.[9]

For Rose, philosophy must stay in this aporetic breach, the middle, between the potentiality and actuality of the world where its effectivity is at stake and often in peril (*Broken Middle* xi). Rose explores her experience of terror and ruin in these late books, but rather than resisting her cancer or lamenting it as condemning her philosophical projects to an untimely end, she is able to convert it (and the faith which it brings her) finally into a form of resolution, of completed mourning.

III. Time and Place

Alar situates its reflections on individual life and death within a larger history. The flow of time and the rivers of death encircle these poems. Charon comes to take the living away in 'Au Hasard Godfrey Cambridge'; his

> ferry comes in daylight, midwise invisible,
> in a white halation playing back its chains
> as yokelore, living memory,
> chuckle-headed phantom of a ship becoming ashes.

The chains of history are a kind of 'yokelore', linking living memory to the past. Critics of the Norman Yoke (including John Warr, the Civil War pamphleteer who 'sings equity' and the privileges of the people to independence in 'Broca's Fold') attributed the alienation of their Saxon freedoms to William I; the English, a conquered people, then conquered the Irish. The 'ship becoming ashes' is also the coffin ship on which Irish émigrés sailed to America. That long and perilous passage may be referenced in the proverb which serves as epigraph to the book: 'is giorra an bóthar soir ná an bóthar siar', or 'the road east is shorter than the road west'. The voyage to Liverpool, from which many of those ships sailed to America, was a less traumatic and radical rupture than the voyage to New York; but this journey to a new history and new world is also longer than ceding to death, putting your feet up in the east, or in Prynne's poem 'rising now / in the east or wherever'. The text wanders through this *Abendland*, the evening land of shadow and starlight, but also the west, the Occident, with its dark history. Ireland's troubles, from the Ascendancy, the Elizabethan injunction to 'hang the harpers and burn the harps', to the Irish Volunteers parading in 1779 on Dublin's College Green and the food riots in Bantry during the Famine, contribute a larger elegiac structure to *Alar*, which was published on the 150th anniversary of Black '47. Death is inscribed on Ireland's history; but it also transforms the narratives of living and mourning, temporality and space, in the elegy for Rose and the other elegiac texts in *Alar*.

'Patience in the Mines' opens with a description of its time and place: 0° Longitude, London. It is a soliloquy spoken at the Royal Observatory at Greenwich, set on a hill above the 'naval college'. Zero degrees longitude: this line is a centering point for the organisation and standardisation of human time. The middle line of the earth can be compared to the distal line of the human body, its mean. 'True Iodine' refers to the 'distal picnic' on Henrietta Lacks' cells in labs around the world. Marking how the triunity of city, soul and body are pervaded with each other, 'Patience in the Mines' begins with the description of rain falling 'over the line / of middle life': over the meridian which marks Greenwich *mean time*, over the line or thread of Rose's middle life or 'half-life' which has been cut, and over the death which attacked the distal line of her body.

The 'now' of the imperium's distal line which displaces all the earth's other presents, is belied in the poem by the diurnal cycle, those nocturnal 'nows' which give way in traditional elegiac fashion to tomorrow's sun. Pastoral elegies such as Milton's 'Lycidas' are timed according to the rising and setting sun, symbol of the redemptive powers of nature. Rose herself celebrated the cycle of bacchanalian revel and repose, of active passion and the grief of sleep. In its last section, Nolan's poem 'would sing that music now to darken', to prevent the irresistible rise of the sun. The poem opens with the observatory gripped by 'cadmium vapour'. This bright chemical flame, used in arc lamps, burns indefinitely, and returns us also to the sodium street lights which light the 'brief night' of Prynne's poem 'Against Hurt'. While an eternal chemical flame might seem an obvious metaphor for the memory of the dead, the site of this poem emphasizes the need for darkness, for the work of mourning. The exchange of day and night allows astronomers to study the stars and the philosopher to study a city reconstituting itself in the darkness of mourning, but London is gripped in a perpetual half-light. For the astronomer, appearance offers proof of the existence of the thing itself; but the Royal Observatory at Greenwich is located at the outskirts of a city whose light pollution makes detailed observation of the skies impossible. This location symbolizes the limitations of post-modern philosophy: surrounded by the unjust city, it cannot provide that vision of potentiality through knowledge of actuality which Rose describes as the broken middle.

The second line describes these as 'spaces there is no bearing', in reference perhaps to Rose's account of her agoraphobia following the breakup of her mother's marriage, her fear of the market, that 'public, articulate space, space full of interconnections' (*Love's Work* p. 123). There is no 'bearing' also because the women struck with ovarian cancer cannot bear children or finally their own pathology. This reference to childbirth, and to stoic acceptance of suffering, returns to a theme of *Alar* as a whole: birth and termination, death and death-before-life. The poem 'Third Milk Directive from the Sun' sings 'my has-been brothers and sisters', 'the ones I dream of when I turn // to the Madonna of homely subincisions'. This poem refers to a 'Carol' who 'cradles a rock, // a Pontius Pilate for non-neonates'. In 1997, when this volume was published, US Senator Carol Moseley-Braun co-sponsored a bill to place limited restrictions on late-term abortions, in response to the stricter provisions of HR1122, known as the 'partial birth abortion ban'. Carol gives way to caroling in the poem; the Madonna of the subincision, of the scar, yields to living music which is 'decussated' in 'Patience in the Mines'. Nolan refers there to the 'clinic', and then to 'wrongful life'. This phrase recalls the 'damaged life' of Adorno's *Minima Moralia* but is also an ironic inversion of the better-known legal term 'wrongful death'. 'Wrongful life' has been used to describe those cases where doctors fail to diagnose in utero disabling conditions which would have led parents to terminate a pregnancy if they had been better informed. In these cases, life itself is considered a kind of 'damage' over which patients and/or their parents can sue the medical establishment. Nolan may be alluding to Rose's confessions in *Love's Work* about her squint and her dyslexia, and the problematic relationship with both her parents and with text which these disabilities express. But the 'wrongful life' is also one celebrated by Rose: 'If I am to stay alive, I am bound to continue to get love wrong, all the time, but not to cease wooing, for that is my life affair, *love's work*' (p. 99).

Nolan's elegy commemorates Rose's scholarly commitment to Hegel in its epigraph, 'das jetzt ist die Nacht', 'the now is the night', taken from Hegel's *Phenomenology of Spirit*, §95-96. Hegel proposes an experiment to test the truth of a sense-certainty: to write down the observation that 'now is night'. Looking back at this inscription by the light of day, we must admit that its truth 'has become stale'. The written 'now' preserves itself in the face of changing time, indifferent to day and night, and is universal only by virtue of that indifference. The value of these observations to Nolan's nocturnal elegy is obvious. The persistence of the now, indifferent not only to the passage of time but also to the passing away of people, is forced into a paradoxical relation with the memorializing activity of the poem, amended in its second version to use the present tense ('my shoes fill / with blood each time it rains'). In contrast to this *'nunc fluens'*, the flowing now which makes time, there is also a *'nunc stans'*, the now that stays or stands and makes eternity, according to Boethius (*De Trinitate* iv). Walter Benjamin, in his essay 'On the Concept of History', describes history as 'the subject of a construction whose site is not homogeneous, empty time, but time filled by the now-time', the *Jetztzeit* or *nunc stans*.[10] Nolan invokes Benjamin's essay in the elegy for Roy Cohn, where he writes: 'across the glass Roy sit and wait, the retrovirus Angelus Novus now for years to come, never less than sure how long each love, what fears diurnal'. Cohn was made after his death into a character in Tony Kushner's *Angels in America*, but the reference here is to the Paul Klee painting which Benjamin owned and discussed in his essay. Propelled by the storm of progress which mounts skyward as a pile of debris, this angel of history 'would like to stay, awaken the dead, and make whole what has been smashed'. In contrast to the powerless angel, Benjamin affirms the power of the historian to fan 'the spark of hope in the past'—an urgent task of backwards redemption of the now, which can only be completed by that historian 'who is firmly convinced that *even the dead* will not be safe from the enemy if he is victorious'. Turning the tables on the inquisitor, Nolan's unpleasant text makes the dead Cohn unsafe, a symbol of the conservative prosecution of the socialist possibility which even now sits in the germ line of American politics, extinguishing all hope of a political order founded on justice.

While the retrovirus transcribes its DNA into that of its host, a 'revertant' mutation is a return to an original state. The virus symbolizes how human action inscribes its consequences on the future, its 'fold in generation' ('True Iodine' and 'Broca's Fold'). The revertant mutation by contrast makes the disappearance of the living look like a wish to obliterate the harm we do:

> Then we are gone, as a body of dusk fades onto water.
> Time folds in revertant whiteface. Poor blood,
> to stand so still, to pity the dark half of whiteness
> over the land.

These lines, from 'Au Hasard Godfrey Cambridge', observe dusk fading—perhaps as we look west, over the ocean at dawn. The diurnal cycle folds time in on itself, the dark returning to the original whiteness which has signified death and disease throughout this text. As the night passes in the Rose elegy, 'The ploughs of spring / rise quick above the season band of / equity harrowed out of time.' The constellations, as images of heroes, and the individual stars—would I were steadfast as thou art—provide a model for survival, for constancy beyond death. The 'equity' they harrow out of time is also that which John Warr sings in 'Broca's Fold': the fundamental equity and liberty of all humans, which intellectual and political corruption prevents us achieving, comparable to 'the equity / of longing' from Prynne's poem 'Song in Sight of the World' (*Poems* 77).

Instead of equity, we live in a state of war: the wars which split the night over Sarajevo, the war which 'speaks in the name of tongues', the violent nature of our 'wrongful life'. He continues, 'How we live is tele- / metry, love of the common curb'. Telemetry, the communication of information over distances—relays of streaming data from space—represents how isolation in the post-modern city has replaced friendship and the unity of the *gens*. The 'common curb' replaces the 'common likeness' discovered in friendship. Nolan writes in 'Au Hasard Godfrey Cambridge', 'when life for like is unlike / and likeness still, it is you we love'. These lines are difficult to interpret; they imply that the lifelike, whose blood 'stands so still' and has become the *nature mort* of 'still-life', is unlike the living; that premise of substitution (like for like) cannot apply to life itself; and that the *you*, loved, departed, is both like and unlike us, the living. But in 'Patience in the Mines', since 'our idiom for past love flies / to graze the links of difference', 'we are friends, beggars for enmity in sameness'. The post-modernist declares us to be linked (chained together) by *differance* in language and the unknowability of the Other, generating 'enmity in sameness'. This is in marked contrast to Rose, or to Prynne in his own way, who seek a return to the ideal city which governs difference with law, or to a language constituted not by the difference between signs but by their identity with the objects of knowledge.

These concerns transform Nolan's use of those elegiac topoi which express the bereaved writer's isolation and loss of identity: 'I have no name, none to recall my common like'; 'This morning I have no sister'. The destitution of the speaker is not just the loss of a twin, sister and friend. It is also a reflection on the loss of ideal relations between individuals, the polis, and language. Given this catastrophic debasement of the act of naming to an assertion of narcissistic will—will after will this names'—what is the point of poetry? The dead have no name and place; they cannot partake in love's work. But the traditional function of the elegy has been to preserve the name from extinction. Nolan's pun on Rose's name—'a sillion rose / over daylight, turned its shadow deep / in half-life, not to mend'—echoes Hopkins' poem 'The Windhover'.

> No wonder of it: sheer plod makes plough down sillion
> Shine, and blue-bleak embers, ah my dear,
> > Fall, gall themselves, and gash gold-vermilion.

Sillion is an obsolete form of selion, or 'narrow-land', the space in an open field between two furrows; 'a portion of land of indeterminate area', as the OED has it.[11] The turning of the plow, which Giorgio Agamben among others have pointed out is an ancient cognate for the verse line turned into the next, creates this indeterminate space between two shadowed cuts. The 'plod' of the plowman recalls the 'toil' of humanity in Johnson's elegy. A selion can also be a low bank, perhaps the one against which 'once the river broke'. In this elegy it is the Thames, as well as the river of death which overflows its banks, that black river over which 'souls fly' ('An Abhainn Dubh'). The 'blue-bleak embers' of Hopkins' poem remind me of David Hume's response as he lay dying of intestinal cancer to Boswell's insistent query: 'is it not possible that there may be a future state, where we shall all account for our sins?' Hume answered, ''Tis possible that a piece of coal, put upon the fire, will not burn, but to suppose so is not at all reasonable. It is a most unreasonable fancy that we should exist forever.'

Despite the inevitability of burning, the darkness of war, and the false dawns of explosions which streak the sky, the new day is inexorable. The elegy concludes with these settling lines:

> It is not raining now, the great frame lifts
> in bright inviolation: to Phocion
> not here, not rising, sparing least.

'The great frame lifts / in bright inviolation', the rain stops, and the inviolable actuality of the sky cedes to brightness, forcing grief also to yield to hope. The harrow of iron which gripped the earth, breaking it into selion shadows, is lifted from its tracks. The mention of this pacifist Athenian philosopher and naval general directs the reader back to *Mourning Becomes the Law*, which opens with Rose's extended meditation on one of the two paintings by Poussin of Phocion's widow collecting his ashes outside the walls of Athens for reburial. Phocion's ashes are *not here*, for the city navigated by this poem is not Athens, the city founded on law; Rose is not here, not rising again, and the speaker's experience still leaves him in the ambivalence of 'sparing' (a contracted 'despairing?'): he is at least spared some patience; he is spared the least hope. My brother will not listen, my sister is dead, and what of all those people which the Serbian or NATO bombs have not spared? This lamentation outside the walls of an unanswering city watches as the shooting stars of ordinance replace the distant constellations. An elegy not only for Rose but also for those dying in the glow of tracer fire, 'Patience in the Mines' leaves us, as Rose's philosophy does, in the half-light, the unmended, broken middle.

Notes

1   J.H. Prynne, *Poems*, 2nd ed. (Fremantle and Tarset: Fremantle Arts Centre Press and Bloodaxe Books, 2005), p. 49.
2   Keston Sutherland, 'J.H. Prynne and Philology', Unpublished PhD Thesis, University of Cambridge, 2004.
3   Gillian Rose, *Mourning Becomes the Law: Philosophy and Representation* (Cambridge University Press, 1996), p. 10.
4   Ludwig Wittgenstein, *Tractatus Logico-Philosophicus*, trans. D. F. Pears and B. F. McGuiness (London and New York: Routledge, 1961), §5.62
5   Ludwig Wittgenstein, *Philosophical Investigations*, trans. G.E.M. Anscombe (Oxford: Blackwell Publishing, 1958), §96.
6   Gillian Rose, *The Broken Middle: Out of Our Ancient Society* (Oxford: Blackwell Publishing, 1992), p. 159.
7   Gillian Rose, *Love's Work* (London: Chatto and Windus, 1995), p. 65.
8   Kevin Nolan, 'Getting Past Odradek', *Literaria Pragensia* 11.22 (2001): 70–84 (81).
9   Gillian Rose, *Paradiso* (London: Menard Press, 1999), p. 35.
10 Walter Benjamin, 'On the Concept of History', *Selected Writings* vol. 4 1938–1940, trans. Edmund Jephcott et al., ed. Howard Eiland and Michael W. Jennings (Cambridge, MA and London: Belknap Press of Harvard University Press, 2003).
11 There is also a possibility that 'sillion' is Hopkins's version of the French 'sillon' which means 'furrow' and in the plural 'ploughed fields'. 'Sillion' as a version of 'sillon' would certainly chime with the other French words in the poem: 'dauphin' and 'chevalier'. See also Virgil, *Georgics* i.43–6: 'in Spring ... let the ploughshare begin to become brilliant from rubbing against the furrow.' Nolan is not only the contemporary British poet to have used Hopkins to broadly political ends. In 'The Infant and The Pearl', Douglas Oliver wrote of the nation in the depths of Thatcherism that 'In this landscape of chance, all at once a Churchillian / ghosting of blue graced the hills' far clothing, / yet the soil near at hand rotted, and the sillion / reeked.' (II. iii) Re-reading Oliver through Hopkins further illuminates the way the passage from 'The Infant and the Pearl' alludes to England as both an abandoned, unworked land; and a wounded body. (Editor's Note.)

Disobedience:
Collaborative Writing and the Walk Poem

IAN DAVIDSON AND ZOË SKOULDING

> 'Next time I'll travel by dream'
> *Fanny Howe from 'O'Clock'.*

This essay is perhaps not so much about walking as rambling, and how that term might apply in various ways both to local walks that inform our work and to a collaborative, conversational process through which we wrote poems by emailing each other four times a week for approximately two years. Our collaborative work produced a wandering discourse that relied on the chance intersections of two different sets of experience. If some of our contributions to the collaborative writing process arose from walking, and they often did, we were very rarely writing about the same places. We would often respond to each other's lines without having any idea of the context, geographical or otherwise, in which they had been written. This process of step-by-step response to each other's lines, combined with the unpredictability of what might turn up in the inbox, was where the connection between physical and verbal rambling began to emerge.

To walk is to embody experience in a specific place and time; it has both a location and a duration. To write a poem about a walk is to produce a poem that can be read outside the specific experience of the walk; the weather, the vistas, the smells and sounds, the pull on the lungs up hill and the feeling of the thigh bones moving in the pelvis and the arms swinging, can be read in different contexts. The form of the poem, the distribution of the words on the page, might try to simulate walking, whether drifting down the page in short lines or in lines that follow a curve but a walk remains a dialogue between the body and the external physical environment. Yet it is a dialogue in which chance is crucial. No two walks are the same because a walk repeated is always a variation. A walk, like a dream, and like writing collaboratively, is a way of losing control. We have become interested in the different ways in which writing and walking can be ways of ordering the world or of discovering it. A parallel enquiry has concerned the manner in which the disembodied space of email communication relates to the embodied experience of place.

Walking contains within it a contradictory relationship between chance and control. Wandering without intent becomes a process of play and of losing control, walking the same patch repeatedly also becomes a process of taking control, of checking out that things are as they should be and of marking out boundaries of ownership. Moving through space therefore becomes simultaneously a process of discovery and ordering, of experiencing and temporarily taking control of the space produced by the walk. Walking is a spatial practice in which, to use Henri Lefebvre's terminology, the representational space of lived and embodied experience is linked to representations of space. The specific is generalised and the general made specific, whether through maps as larger structures in which the walk takes place or within more general concepts.

Our rambling, a kind of subset of walking which can link the physical experience of the walk and the process of collaborative composition, becomes a rural version of the *dérive*. We live in an area of north Wales where most walks are necessarily rural, and walking round Menai Bridge is not like walking round Paris. Guy Debord said that the rural *dérive* was 'naturally depressing'. However, in contemporary Wales, the distinctions between rural and urban walking are increasingly blurred. We live near the two bridges that connect Anglesey to the mainland and London to the ferry crossing to Ireland. On the mainland side of the Telford Bridge, there is a traffic camera pointing towards Anglesey that transmits live pictures twenty-four hours a day on a BBC website where visitors from around the world post comments. Given this intensity of modern communication and its ability to locate the subject simultaneously in a range of contemporary experiences, it's hard to say where the city ends and the countryside begins. There are other connections that blur relationships between the rural and the urban. Major roads, in particular, provide unbroken links between urban centres, reducing the rural to a space that needs to be crossed between cities. Expressways and motorways are owned and maintained by central government, whereas minor roads and byways are under local control. It is 'illegal' to walk on major roads, and they have to be negotiated in other ways. One cannot therefore 'ramble' freely in the countryside.

There are barriers and boundaries imposed from outside.

The concrete underside of Bont Britannia, a dominant feature of the landscape where we live, carries a European Expressway linking London to Holyhead. It looms out of the woods like a lost fragment of an urban landscape, reminding one of places in Berlin where the disappearance of the Wall suddenly re-routed many of the roads, leaving stranded bridges and lookout towers without a purpose. The brace of stone lions at each end of the bridge is an assertion of empire at one of its extremities, an extra reinforcement of London's grip on the route to Dublin. This grip is further reinforced by a mini 'marble arch' located in Holyhead port, although this road has also been re-routed, leaving the arch stranded at the end of the port and surrounded by a high fence. Since the rebuilding of the bridge in the Seventies, the stone lions have been invisible, except to the walker.

Walter Benjamin's flâneur knew the landscape of Paris through the 'second existence' of historical reading about an intensely documented city that deepens awareness of place. Contemporary 'second existence' for a comparably privileged person is likely to include connections across the globe through electronic systems of communication. The geographer Doreen Massey describes this contemporary spatial experience in terms of 'a simultaneous multiplicity of spaces: cross-cutting, intersecting, aligning with one another, or existing in relationships of paradox or antagonism.'[1] In a culture of simultaneous existences here and elsewhere, one is just as likely to connect one place with another as to dig down through the depths of associations in a single location. Our writing has also been a process of making outward movements within an aesthetic that subordinates the containment and depth of the individual lyric self to an open, interconnected discourse. An extract from one of the poems shows this process at work:

> crushed between his fingers under
> horrible blue skies the view from
> the window out of Blake via
> Ginsberg the scent bog myrtle
>
> from Buddha-clouds the roads
> go south we cried for Kerouac

he kicked off his shoes a small room
disciplines the mind

so across cross firs the view is
down the valley where
ridges meet a series of vees
sighted through where the wall was

she sat beneath her shadow
the shade of an ancient thorn
haw and blackthorn intertwined
dodgy figures grounds for suspicion

hedged in by mathematics
sloes furring the tongue another
stone in the wall numbers coming
loose under your foot

The poem connects a number of texts, and not only those by the
three writers mentioned; we also quote each other's poems: 'horrible
blue skies' refers to a quotation from T. E. Lawrence in Zoë's poem
'Uruk', while the line about Kerouac is a reference to Ian's 'laid by'.
Like the flâneur, we walk with the memory of texts in our heads, so that
the walk can be shaped by them, just as the poem is. The details that
suggest immediate physical experience, like the scent of bog myrtle (a
detail which is 'stolen' from Lee Harwood's 'September Dusk by Nant
Y Gueallt' following a walk Ian took with Lee in the Mountains above
Capel Curig, a walk which also provided the image of the intertwined
hawthorn and blackthorn) and the taste of sloes, are not the experiences
of the same person but are organised as such in the shape of the poem,
so that the poem becomes a re-ordering of experience.

Several months after writing this poem, we decided to make a
film to use in performance. This involved, unusually, going for a walk
together. We went along the Menai Straits, past the place where Zoë
had been picking sloes, and along to the foot of Britannia Bridge, where
we chalked sections of the poem alongside the graffiti and filmed the
words emerging. The poem, in this case, was the occasion for the

walk, although it had grown out of other walks. In Massey's terms, the disembodied space of virtual communication cross-cuts, intersects, and aligns with other spaces as textual and embodied experiences of place are woven together through the chance relations of verbal and physical rambling.

One would not necessarily associate Tom Raworth with the 'walk poem'. Yet in a description of his method of composition in 'A letter to Martin Stannard', he frames the writing of a poem with two excursions punctuated by other events.[2] Raworth talks about returning to his room to 'find' words on an envelope, some of which he then incorporates into the final poem. The 'writing' uses detail and observations from the walk without trying to simulate the experience. The act of walking is that of embodied presence, of a lived experience that is a process of discovery. Writing a poem is a process of arranging language, yet can similarly be a process of discovery, of moving from one word to the next, where the act of writing becomes an embodied lived experience. The poem is not simply a reduction of the concrete experience of the walk to an abstraction which is re-concretised by the reader. Collaborative writing adds another layer of discovery, having to move from the word of your co-writer to the next word, and then stopping in mid stride for them to pick up. If writing collaboratively is like rambling it is as if you're blindfolded for certain sections, and then when you can see again you're in a new location and not entirely sure how you got there. It's like being picked up and put down in a series of points along a trajectory of unknown direction or duration where the past can be reviewed but the future cannot be predicted. Collaborative writing, therefore, is as much an act of reading as it is an act of writing. On receiving a section of the poem, we each have to read it before responding. It is an act of interpretation and an act of discovery.

Yet that act of discovery is not innocent or naïve. We see what we want to see and in the way we want to see it. The selection of the detail to record is itself an interpretative act. In the John James poem 'The Conversation' about walking up Snowdon, ecological concerns come into the first line where 'Snowdon is falling apart', and 'the Zig Zags' (a descriptive name for a path up Snowdon) are held together with wire mesh.[3] The central part of the poem is a reflection on his own Welsh working class background, before returning to address a loved one. James' point is a simple one, that for all its embodied experience, for all the sense of presence of walking up a mountain, other things live coincidentally and in relation to other structures. The poem ends, not with an affirmation of the healing power of nature, but with an evocation to human collectivity through language: 'I see the millions I catch the language/which is the world of all of us/this only place in which we find our happiness or not at all/the end'. The place is not only the place of the walk, its geographical location, or the subjective place of the lyric 'I', but also the general place of 'language' and the specific language of the poem.

Within the collaborative process there is an implicit critique of abstractions of the embodied experience, whether these are maps or conceptual frameworks. That is why we have never planned the direction of a poem before writing it. We have begun each poem as a negotiation of an unmapped space, taking it line by line and putting one foot in front of the other. Where structures emerge, they tend to be as rhythms and patterns that come from repetitions as we get into our stride, not because either one of us has an overhead view. There are good reasons to mistrust maps. In Denise Riley's work, the body orientates itself through the senses, and through specifics, never trusting the information of the general. In 'Pastoral' the mapped perspective is presented, with irony, as masculine:

> Gents in a landscape hang above their lands.
> Their long keen shadows trace peninsulas on fields.[4]

Qazi Rahman's recent and well-publicised research has found evidence that women and gay men are less likely to orient themselves by maps and the points of the compass, as straight men usually do, and more likely to find their bearings through a series of landmarks.[5] Neither of us would want to pursue this idea from an essentialist point of view, but it does suggest that different people might approach walking and writing with varying levels of overview and control. One of Riley's most recognisable walk poems is a tour from the perspective of a male persona. 'Goethe On His Holidays' follows a trajectory through a landscape marked out by specific details:

I and my truthful knapsack will strike out
To backpack through 'this sea-fog snaked on walls,

Wool snagged on slate, lichen-splodged rocks
In spattered chromes, and cadmium flowered gorse'[6]

As the poem continues, the concepts of both 'I' and 'truth' are destabilised through the exploration of colour and perception, so even landmarks are not to be trusted as a way of knowing the world. The idea of striking out implies personal control and agency, but this soon overwhelmed by the effort of interpreting the external world, detail by detail.

In Riley's 'Outside from the start', a collapse of the overhead view is suggested by 'a pale calm page shoots up, opening rapidly / to say I know'.[7] Agency is transferred from the speaker to her surroundings, and the individual is truly 'open to the world' in Merleau Ponty's terms, and no longer self-contained and protected. Don Ihde has described the island navigators of the Pacific, who had no texts or maps but learned songs about particular journeys. The navigator would use the position of his own body as a constant and judge everything else according to it, and the language would change as Riley's does. He would say 'Tahiti is approaching', rather than 'I am nearing Tahiti.'[8] The bird's eye view is a textual view of space and it is a cultural construction belonging to the modern West. Michel de Certeau describes it as enabling one to 'be a solar Eye, looking down like a god'.[9] The process of writing collaboratively has in some ways been a rejection of that perspective. It involves continuous response to a moving and unpredictable textual landscape.

Michel de Certeau compares walking with dreaming, since 'To walk is to lack a place. It is the indefinite process of being absent and in search of a proper.'[10] where the 'proper' refers to a distinct, defined location that can be unsettled by both walks and dreams. Alice Notley's collection *Disobedience* is not exactly a walk poem but its journeys chart the subconscious as an alternative space that disrupts the external Parisian cityscape. In 'Sun is Very Near Hot and Buttockslike', the figure of Dante appears in cartoon form suggesting that this is the beginning of a visionary journey but one which resists forward propulsion by connecting outward to real and dreamed places.[11] It begins in 'the Needles

Pharmacy/Mortuary', cuts to another dream of a 'white / bridge from nowhere to nowhere' then to 'the "real", in the métro"'. Dreams, like walks, make arbitrary connections. The logic of 'real' space, the fact we that we expect disconnected sights and impressions to lie between two points at the beginning and end of a journey, gives a logic to the walk poem. Notley's anti-programme of 'disobedience' resists the shape and purpose of linearity and time. To write from dreams, as to write from a walk, is a way of losing control over the writing process. For Notley, as for Walter Benjamin's flâneur, 'every street is precipitous. It leads downward'.[12] Her preoccupation with the underground and with caves is a way of getting underneath the readable surface of the city, of evading the control of others as well as refusing to take it herself.

This essay, written collaboratively by passing ideas backwards and forwards, has itself been something of a ramble. The process of collaboration in writing the poems that the essay describes and refers to was, at the time of writing, purposely unreflective. As we said before, we didn't talk about it, but kept the work in the virtual space of e-mail. Writing this essay, which follows on from a dialogue published in *New Welsh Review* in which we discussed methods and procedures, has compelled us to place that process in broader contexts. The further development of a metaphoric relationship between writing and walking, and its application to the collaborative writing process, has opened up a series of connections, both individually and collectively, between approaches to public and private space and the relationship between writing and the philosophical, literary and social contexts of our own writing. One's way of doing things, particularly of writing poems, however explicitly open or experimental, becomes one way of operating amongst others, and self imposed boundaries are revealed and questioned.

Notes

[1] Doreen Massey, *Space, Place and Gender* (Oxford: Blackwell Publishing, 1994) 3.

[2] In Nate Dorward, ed, *Removed for Further Study: The Poetry of Tom Raworth* (Willowdale, Ont.: The Gig, 2003), 204–206.

[3] John James, in *On Wales* (Skald, 2003) 24.

[4] Denise Riley, *Selected Poems* (London: Reality Street Editions, 2000) 64.

[5] Qazi Rahman, Davinia Andersson and Ernest Govier, 'A Specific Sexual Orientation-Related Difference in Navigation Strategy,' *Behavioral Neuroscience*, 2005 Vol.119(1) 311–316.

[6] Denise Riley, *Selected Poems* (London: Reality Street Editions, 2000) 105.

[7] ibid, 97.

[8] Don Ihde, *Postphenomenology: Essays in the Postmodern Context* (Illinois: Northwestern University Press, 1993) 27.

[9] Michel de Certeau, *The Practice of Everyday Life* (Berkeley: University of California Press, 1984) 92.

[10] Michel de Certeau, ibid., 103.

[11] Alice Notley, *Disobedience* (New York: Penguin Books, 2001) 8.

[12] Walter Benjamin, *The Arcades Project*, trans. Howard Eiland and Kevin McLaughlin (Cambridge, MA., and London: Belknap Press, Harvard University Press, 1999) 416.

Falling Towards Each Other: Occasions of Elegy

John Hall

I walk down in the evening to the graveyard of Holy Trinity Church. The light is fading and there is a hint of Autumn (Fall) in the air. I am reflecting on forms of loss, especially deaths, and the forms and practices of words—and of other 'texts'—that 'we' use to define and negotiate these. This is something I do anyway. I am not unusual in those strands of my reflection which are to do with loss and death; 'everybody' does it. Only those interested in writing and / or the precise forms of social and psychic processes which deal with loss are likely to combine the two strands of reflection and put them up against each other. On this occasion I am responding to an invitation for some writing and so the reflection is occasioned and occasional. And actually the walk is not *down* to the graveyard; it is *up*.[1] That 'down' is already, perhaps, elegiac. And that present tense, where did that fall from? Actually the walk was two evenings ago as I write this sentence.[2]

The building of Holy Trinity was severely damaged by arson some years ago. The last time I was here was after the fire for the funeral of a friend, Peter Knight, who taught Physics in school and wrote poems. The ceremony included a reading of poems. They were all his poems, offered in a doubly double move, *from* him back *to* him, and—through the attention of congregated friends, colleagues and relatives—*to* something *from* him that marked both *loss* and *survival* at one and the same time. There is always this second doubleness attached to the deaths of those whose business it is to leave traces which sustain a present tense after their deaths. Of course there are also all those traces in the form of photographs which Susan Sontag and others have argued are already epitaphs. Those photographs, some of which are framed monumentally, haunt with their temporal ambiguity, ghostly presences of loss—loss either of youth, or situation, or life.[3] Has anyone left instructions to have all photographs of themselves burnt after their death?

The poems read in the roofless church at Peter Knight's funeral were not specifically written for the occasion of mourning—they were not, in other words, elegies. Though recited here on an occasion that marked the death of their author, they were chosen to celebrate the quality of the man and his writing: *this is what we have lost*. There were people who had been very close to him who were weeping. And there are poems—music, of course, even more so—that could take up that weeping, share it and shape it in lachrymae and lamentations, a modulated ritual procedure to bring people together in topically acknowledged forms of grief.

> Ye sacred Muses, race of Jove,
> Whom Music's lore delighteth,
> Come down from crystal heav'ns above
> To earth, where sorrow dwelleth,
> In mourning weeds, with tears in eyes:
> Tallis is dead, and Music dies.[4]

This occasion, by contrast, allows differing investments in loss and proceeds through a mosaic ritual of differing participations.

After years of not hearing William Byrd's elegy I had playing through my head two of the repeated phrases: 'Come down' and 'Tallis is dead'. Tempo, iteration, tone, duration: it takes time and repetition to mourn. My version of *Ye sacred muses*, on crackly vinyl with brittle sound, lasts three minutes and twenty seconds.[5] Four phrases are repeated: 'Come down', 'In mourning weeds', 'Tallis is dead' and 'Music dies'. The last two lines are repeated with all their internal repetitions, with a third and final 'Music dies'. Music has died five times, and survives. In this slow, extended and repeated time, grief can be joined and given a collective shape. Is the elegy a lyric account prompted by an occasion? Or is it part of the shape of an occasion, a component of ceremony, designed to perform mourning? And what ceremony do I perform when I listen to it on my own at home, by virtue of a newer and more mobile technology of memory that allows a displaced mourning, a grieving for a loss—perhaps indefinable—that the mourning itself might or might not name? And I would want to generalise out to a larger notion of occasion and even to trouble the question with another, both political and anthropological: *whose occasion?*

The Oxford English Dictionary gives as the etymology for *occasion*: 'ad. L. *occasion-em* falling (of things) towards (each other)'.[6] It is not just the *things* that fall towards each other, though there is always, I would say, a sense of conjuncture or convergence that marks something as an 'occasion', even for those with their attention on the 'everyday'. It is also that occasions are marked incidents that cause certain people to fall together. Many are set, as though permanently, by calendars. And I see from the Oxford English Dictionary that the etymology of calendar is the Latin word for an account book—accounts were due on the *calends* of each month. Rent day. Pay day. These are occasions.

Many of these calendric occasions are now routinely marked with the exchange of texts and images in the form of cards: for example, birthdays, Christmas, New Year (and its eve), St Valentine's day. Others, such as solstices, equinoxes, new and full moons, are not (yet) marked with the routine exchange of cards but are often the occasion for poems. Some of these are grand dispersed occasions in which the texts can be ephemeral simply because they will be repeated—or at least variants will be. I have become very taken with these opportunities for textual production and circulation, with their lines into established expectations; texts can be used to cause or maintain a falling together through the formalising or ritualising of formulaic exchanges, like the exchange of gifts. It is far too limiting to see these as genres of texts only: they are genres of cultural exchange in which the formal properties of the texts may or may not be wholly fixed. Participants may be mesmerised by the strictly regulated formalism of the required texts or may, at another extreme, become thoughtfully pragmatic and functionalist: *what is it we should be doing here and what text will do that job?*

These questions are anthropological before they are literary or, in the thick of pragmatics, they are both sociable and ethical, and will inevitably raise further questions about the 'occasion' of any textual event. What are the complex dynamics of the falling together of texts, events and people, such that certain texts can simply signal that this is an occasion of such-and-such a kind and that certain kinds (*genres*) of occasion can signal the need for appropriate textual behaviour?

The role of news media in this signalling has been much noticed recently, in responding to occasions of death in which it is decided that there is no stance for a commentary that is not complicit in the occasion: the death of the daughter-in-law of the British queen; the destruction of the World Trade Centre in New York; and, as I write, two young girls in Cambridgeshire whose murders become an exemplary loss for 'all of us'. As with commentaries on grand state events, including coronations, the commentators become MCs of a pervasive rhetorical—and imbricated—layer of proceedings.

Andrea Brady's recent article in *Quid*(9), focusing on the deployment of grief to regulate difference and commentary, put the questions very forcibly: in a world of rhetorical interactions, were you pushed or did you fall?[7] The occasion that she considered—the aftermath of the events of September 11th 2001—is one whose rhetorical community was immediately constructed through news media and those with access to using them as sites of address as universal, as the community of 'the world'. That this particular occasion could be repeated, that is a fearful political question, whose provisional answer is provided on behalf of the 'world' through military action, threat of military action, intelligence, diplomacy, tireless rhetorical and ideological activity. Unlike, say, a marriage or the entirely predictable death of those near the ends of their lives, this is something 'we' do not want repeated. If its rhetorical management is to be effective, though, it must *repeat* (be citational, re-enact key elements of previous performances) and be *repeatable*, bringing together previous responses to grand scale disasters, to deaths of those *not* expected to be at the end of their lives, to horrific crimes and to times of hostility when the enemy can only be understood as 'evil'.[8]

Part of the rhetoric of an *exceptional* occasion is just that, a rhetoric of exception: *this has never happened before*. Available for such, perhaps, are genres of the monstrous, the grotesque. But otherwise, it is because these occasions are repeatable, are themselves generic, that there can be genres of speech acts; it is because there are genres of speech acts that the occasions can be repeated, modulated, orchestrated.[9] Any number of *performances* can derive from a social *competence*. In this sense an occasion is always an occasion of an Occasion and participation marks more than itself.[10] There are rules, and one of the rules, as Andrea Brady illustrates, may be that participation is not optional.

So in these terms there is Death, which stalks 'us all', and there are the deaths of friends, relations, public figures, people in our own trades, perhaps, whom we admire. Each of these deaths is part of an already formed narrative and we deal with it as best we can, caught somewhere between loss, memorialising (often this is of an already lost younger version of the person), frustration at unfinished business, care of those even closer, juggling perhaps with any re-positioning that is a consequence of the death, and with what happens to our own view of mortality, of transience.

Elegy deals with mournfulness as well as with mourning. As form and modality, elegy can respond to sense of loss and mortality and can articulate a relationship with the literal dead. It can also be a specific form of memorialising through grief, through affective and/or substantive articulation of loss. Such is Byrd on Tallis. 'Music is dead,' he has his singers sing in a wonderful demonstration that it is not.

J. H. Prynne's *Shadow Songs*, where 'glorious dead' invokes the genre of war memorial, seem to me to work across and away from a sense of loss, and at the same time to sing in its shadows.[11] There is no named death in the poems, just the glorious dead. Nor do they mark an established occasion, so far as I know, for remembrance of the glorious dead. And where I encounter them is not as part of any shared ceremony ('Only the procession is halted') but on the page of a book that can be visited at any time, because I own a copy. I need enter no public space, except for the space that the poem itself constructs, to join a ceremony of meditation. This is itself an occasion, a variant of the occasion of individualised reading, like listening to Byrd on my own. I don't feel that I understand it. Sometimes, perhaps, the 'lovely harm' of reading is the lost company of those signally not present to the act of reading. I am talking about a kind of text, not wishing yet to generalise: how can a private reading be elegiac? Mournful, perhaps, or melancholic, in Freud's (or his translator's) sense of the term?

Like Byrd's elegy on Tallis, *Shadow Songs* combine a grammatical sense of indirect imperative with all the implications of 'come down':

> And let Nightingale come
> down from the hills.

and

> And if the dead know this,
> coming down into the dark, why should
> they be stopped?[12]

The poem also carries that already cited troubling oxymoron, 'lovely harm' ('the years with their lovely harm'): elegy can't remove harm but can, perhaps, render it 'lovely'.[13] It is, I would say, a charm *against* loss: the dead can walk barefoot on the earth. John Riley, another poet whose death was untimely, also engaged often with this paradox.

Recent secular practices of memorial are more likely to specify the dead, using grounded memories, with an obligation of a truth to the person even if that crosses the taboo of 'about the dead, nothing unless it's good'. *This is the person in the round. I remember their faults with affection. To ignore these would be to wrong them.* William Carlos Williams's 'To Ford Madox Ford in Heaven', playing on the title of Ford's *On Heaven*, is a deliberate example, making only ambivalent allowance for elegiac cadences or modal gestures to the sublime (the conceit of heaven), instead using a direct form of address as of honesty to a friend loved with reservation:

> A heavenly man you seem to me now, never
>   having been for me a saintly one.

and

> Provence, the fat assed Ford will never
>   again strain the chairs of your cafés
> pull and pare for his dish your sacred garlic,
>   grunt and sweat and lick
> his lips.[14]

Ford had already offered the ambivalence that allows heaven to *come down* into the secular environment of earth, and so Williams can, in what is probably another tradition of elegies, borrow the effects of a cosmology from which he is at least at one remove. In another of Williams's elegies on a writer, 'An Elegy for D.H. Lawrence', the ironic term is 'love' rather than 'heaven' ('men driven not to love / but to the ends of the earth') and there are, as in the performed version of Byrd's elegy on Tallis, repeated variants of the statement that the named person is dead.[15] There is no redundancy in such repetition. The first step in responding to a death is perhaps to verify that it has happened; the second perhaps is to speak the death—for each verifier to say it: Lawrence is dead. The first is witness; the second participation in utterance. And the 'utterance' can be transposed into ceremony—even silence—provided that the ceremony clearly performs the statement: the person named is dead. This is what funerals do: (i) indeed the named person is dead—look!; (ii) this is the named person who is dead. And then mourning can begin.[16]

In the graveyard of Holy Trinity Church the recent gravestones convey, in their brevity, a variation on a few themes. One—an obvious one—is the marking of a life through the specificity of dates of birth and death, to create that poignant narrative of a supposedly unique chronology, most poignant when the death was of a young person ('Aged 2 ½ years; So precious') or, in one instance in the graveyard, where husband and wife had died within days of each other. The gap between these deaths was only eleven days and those responsible for commissioning the inscription had arranged for the two-liner from Sir Henry Wotton to be included:

> She first deceased, he for a little tried
> To live without her, liked it not and died.
> Sir Henry Wotton 1568–1639

This gravestone is a memorial not only to two individuals but also to their marriage (and of course to Wotton, also given his dates). As a naïve visitor to the graveyard I was not ready for how prevalent a theme this one of domestic relationship was. Many of these dead are remembered as husbands, wives, grandparents—less frequently, of course, as sons and daughters. The loss implied in all these cases is a domestic and familial one: a beloved and exemplary family member is dead; here they lie. In no case that I saw (admittedly only a few rows) was any other social position, such as a trade or occupation, cited. It is as though it is the repeatability of *family* that makes these losses public: the ready identification of family with family, which shapes so much contemporary public grieving. In the still prevalent schematic cosmology of *up*, *down* and *here*, family and home are *here*. 'Here' is also, by extension, 'earth', which can be set off against 'eternity', as Emily Dickinson does in 'The Bustle in a house':

The Bustle in a House
The Morning after Death
Is solemnest of industries
Enacted upon Earth —

The Sweeping up the Heart
And putting Love away
We shall not want to use again
Until Eternity.[17]

Loss is not stated as such in the graveyard, though memorials of this kind always mark the place of loss, and do so again in a double function captured in the phrase, 'lest we forget': they are sites of memory *and* commitments to remember (wards *against* the fearful loss that is forgetfulness). Memorial is seldom taken as read but is doubled with redundancy: *IN LOVING MEMORY; CHERISHED MEMORIES.* Loss is approached more directly through the word 'missed', always coupled with 'sadly', with its implication of an emotional aim that has lost its object, whose object may just have gone missing.[18] The epitaphs move in on the generic business of elegies, it seems to me, with this declaration of sorrow or lack. The occasion of an elegy is the period of mourning, in which grief is a process with a duration (in some societies, carefully regulated through dress code and restrictions on activity; in Freudian psychoanalysis, a process with a discernible narrative).[19] A gravestone is intended to be permanent; using Freud's much discussed distinction you could say a statement of sorrow on a gravestone—fixed rather than re-iterated—is to commit to melancholia and to refuse mourning its due process. I wouldn't for a minute want to suggest that this is actually what happens; only that the domestication of the public marker is also a temporal domestication. These are the dead Thomas Gray wanted to bring into the privileged domain of the glorious dead, the domain of those who occasion not just epitaph but also elegy.

The last theme from these gravestones is the notion of peaceful rest, usually through the familiar formulation of 'REST IN PEACE'. 'Rest' allows for ambiguity: refreshment, remains, and—another imperative—'stay there'. Where the life of the dead person had been troubled, particularly through painful illness at its end, then there is a domestic and curative poignancy: just rest there; let nothing trouble you. What is invoked is the euphoric emptying of sleep. Peace is there to ward off the anxiety of bad dreams that Hamlet feared. It seems to me that this term skirts around the association of death with the sublime without ever losing the domestic (and therefore profane but literarily touching) gesture of the soothing of the brow. How long can soothing take?

I keep the company
of the articulate dead, whose remaining
purpose is to talk to us
of their living. I also keep the company of the living,
naturally, otherwise would not be interested
in the dead. I listen to each
and talk back.   no one
will silence any of us, because we talk
in the company of the dead
with those who live
now or at any time.   don't ask me
why this is.

This is the first section of a piece called *Apple Poems* which I wrote in about 1968 and then lost. I recovered it recently after talking with a friend, who had known the poem at the time, of its loss. No, she said, she had a copy. Meanwhile the opening statement, 'I keep the company / of the articulate dead' was never 'lost' because I remembered it. I wanted to make good the loss by writing out from that opening.

When Alaric Sumner (13/3/1948–24/3/2000) died, I put in the place of his loss this:

THE
ARTIC-
ULATE
DEAD
WHERE
EVERY
EAR

And had very much in mind too Douglas Oliver (14/9/1937–21/4/2000) and Barry MacSweeney (17/7/1948–9/5/2000). I was unable to attend a memorial gathering at Dartington for Alaric but produced, to be shown in my absence, an animated Powerpoint piece, whose colour, scale and tempo are missing from this representation just as the setting is from the Byrd elegy. It began with the above and then:

PERHAPS · IT · EASES · THE · LIVING · IF · THE
DEAD · STAY · STILL · ALARIC · IN · AND
OUT · OF FRAME · A · LURE · TO · THE
LIVING · ALWAYS TO · AN · OTHER · PLACE
ALL · WAYS · ALARMED · RESTLESSNESS
HELPS · LIVING · TONGUES · TO · MOVE · SO

September 2002

Notes

[1] This word 'actually' is for me, and perhaps others, a memorial marker of the poet, Douglas Oliver, who died in 2000. When I hear it used, including by myself, in a particular way, I remember him and the part the word played in his speaking. It was for him, I think, another kind of marker—it marked the entry into the register of authoritative explanation.

[2] See Gillian Rose on the 'pathos of syntax' in *Mourning Becomes the Law: Philosophy and Representation* (Cambridge: Cambridge University Press, 1996) pp. 125–126

[3] Certain kinds of sound recordings can have the same effect. I have just moved offices at work and have changed telephone numbers. Alaric Sumner, whose sudden death in March 2000 so shocked friends, colleagues and students, must have been the last person to have used the number because when I set about changing the message on the answering facility what I heard was: *hello this is Alaric*. For a second or two this was a living voice, and consequently it was as though for a second or two I had to re-enact a mourning. I take up aspects of this theme below.

[4] William Byrd *Elegy on the death of Thomas Tallis*, 23rd November, 1585.

[5] Mary Thomas, John Whitworth et al: *An Anthology of Elizabethan and Restoration Vocal Music* (London: Saga, 1964)

[6] Oxford English Dictionary (CD-ROM Version 2, 1999).

[7] 'Grief Work in a War Economy', in *Quid*(9) (Gonville and Caius College, Cambridge, 2002).

[8] Are most of the best known elegies in this category? Mahler's *Songs for the Death of Children* were not allowed in the house when our sons were young.

[9] This phrase is intended to evoke the title of M. M. Bakhtin's *Speech Genres and Other Late Essays* (Austin: University of Texas Press, 1986, 1996) and also J. L. Austin's notion of speech acts which has been so usefully put to work by, among others, Judith Butler.

[10] The title of one of John Riley's poems is *A Birthday Poem / For One person, and Hence for Others*; John Riley *The Collected Works* (Wirksworth and Leeds: Grossteteste Press, 1980) pp. 93–94.

[11] J. H. Prynne *Poems* (Fremantle and Newcastle upon Tyne: Folio / Fremantle Arts Centre Press and Bloodaxe Books, 1999) p.81. I hear Thomas Campion's *Follow Your Saint* when I read these 'songs'.

[12] Is that what a prayer is, a necessarily indirect imperative? When dealing with death, who is giving the orders? Gillian Rose touches on this in the last section of *Mourning Becomes the Law* (cited above).

[13] 'Heavenly Hurt, it gives us –
     We can find no scar,'   ('There's a certain Slant of light...')
     Emily Dickinson (ed. Thomas H. Johnson), *The Complete Poems* (London and Boston: Faber and Faber, 1975) p.118.

[14] William Carlos Williams *The Collected Later Poems* (London: MacGibbon and Kee, 1965) pp. 60–61.

[15] '...poor Lawrence dead ... Dead now... Remember, now, Lawrence is dead ... Poor Lawrence / dead... ... Lawrence has passed unwanted...' William Carlos Williams *The Collected Earlier Poems* (New York: New Directions, 1938, 1951) pp. 361-364.

[16] It happened that Douglas Oliver and Anthony Barnett visited Dartington, I think for a reading, just before John Riley's funeral in early November 1978. We travelled up to Leeds together for the funeral. Doug told us that he had just been reading something which explained why it was important to attend a funeral: it was so that you really know that the person is dead. I can't now ask him if he can remember what it was he had been reading.

[17] Emily Dickinson, cited above, p.498.

[18] Oxford English Dictionary, under verb[1] 16. 'To perceive with regret the absence or loss of, to feel the want of...'

[19] Sigmund Freud, 'Mourning and Melancholia', in Volume XIV of the Standard edition, translated and edited by James Strachey (London: The

Hogarth Press, 1957); pp. 243–258); also in the same volume, 'Thoughts for the Times on War and Death' and 'On Transience'; see also, though I would not want to suggest that her work belongs within the category of 'Freudian psychoanalysis', Gillian Rose's *Mourning Becomes the Law*, cited above—especially p.35—which argues that the procedures (and these of course include tempo) of mourning are political, 'become the law'.

Poetry and Spirituality:
Lectio Divina and The Patience of Angels

Sarah Law

Lectio Divina: (Latin, 'divine/holy reading'). Attention to the scriptures (or occasionally a spiritual text) in an attitude of prayer and devotion, leading to communion with God. It is thus in contrast to exegesis seeking meaning of the text. It is fundamental to the Rule of St Benedict and to monastic life.

The Oxford Dictionary of World Religions

The connections between spirituality and writing have always fascinated me. I wrote my postgraduate thesis on modernist women writers and the way they spoke about mysticism. I looked at how novelists like May Sinclair (the first to use stream-of-conscious technique) and Dorothy Richardson stretched the boundaries of language to approach the barely articulate, the unexpected, the spiritual. I found my way back to the medieval mystics, their (often female-authored) poetic stream of visions, symbol, and dialogue with a frequently sensual Divine. Then I found my way forward to the diverse world of contemporary poetry. I now spend much of my time teaching the reading and writing of it. The following reflects my interests and makes no claim to be either objective or inclusive.

In this essay I would like to explore some of the affinities between poetry and spirituality. In particular, I would like to pay attention to the practice of reading attentively, 'reading differently', that both traditional spiritual practice and poetry with any real depth invite. Spiritual reading encompasses 'the literal, the moral and the mystical', declares Origen.[1] And as a touchstone I would like to recall the spiritual tradition of *Lectio Divina*: the slow, careful absorption of a (spiritual) text which opens up sound and image and space as well as grammatical linear construction. It is a way of patience, rather than complexity. It is a way of being open to revelation rather than applying a reading agenda. It is, perhaps, a route towards mysticism.

Definitions of mysticism, however, are notoriously difficult to unravel. I do not have the space here to sift through the many attempts, ancient and modern, to clarify what is essentially a mysterious experience, something beyond the normal bounds of language or logic. The philosopher William James, writing in 1902, described such experiences as ineffable: something with conviction, something akin to a spiritual/creative leap which can best be expressed through accumulation of image, symbol, or sound, rather than linguistic logic. Evelyn Underhill's comprehensive *Mysticism*, first published in 1911, is still in print today: she sees mysticism as a completely universal phenomena, outside the context of cultural and historical difference. This is an academically dubious position. But I do find it fascinating that various aspects of poetry, contemporary poetry, explore the same aspects of language and vision as do the mystics, particularly the medieval mystics. I am not suggesting that secretly all poets are mystics, and all poems an expression of this—although a sizeable number of poets clearly are drawn to spirituality. But I would like to suggest that it is helpful to consider the connections between these ways of reading and writing. Concentrated poetic texts sometimes hint at the limitations of language itself. They engender in the reader a greater awareness of both limitation and mystery. In our secular age of speed and sound-bite this is an uncommon but arguably vital pursuit.

To begin with the basics. What are the ostensible similarities between spirituality and poetry? The following observations are generalities only but serve as a starting point. Poetry—like written prayer—is an intense, concentrated form of language. It is often short and lyrical, particularly in our impatient culture which likes a brief poetic piece rather than a vast Keatsian realm. It is often personal writing, not necessarily confessional, but able to consider the inner implications of external settings or events. Of course, poetry may have a fictional 'I', a fractured narrative voice or voices, or no narrative voice at all but the common perception remains that poetry is a vehicle for communicating and exploring deep feelings. For these reasons, poetry, like prayer, has an appeal in times of emotional crisis and intensity. Major episodes of loss and celebration prompt the writing and reading of poetry from those who would never normally be amenable to it. Other people, of course, do have the habit of poetry in their bloodstream the way some have the habit of prayer: regard it as *chronos* (the duration of time) rather than *kairos* (a specific time of crisis or salvation). But perhaps we should look again at the basics of the writing on the page.

On the page, liturgical passages, prayers and poetry often look a little like each other. All tend to be shorter than other forms of writing, such as sermon or story. Because there are relatively few words, one can often retain a line or a phrase more easily in the memory, and turn it over and over in meditation, like a bead or worry stone. Different meanings rise to the surface of an image or word the more one ponders. Both can use 'lineation'—the breaking up of a piece of writing into poetic 'lines' on the page. In this way, poems and prayers have an extra form of punctuation—a slight pause at the end of the line. More, they have a setting of stillness surrounding them—the white space on the page. This indicates a context of silence in our reading of them, something which is very much missing from our contemporary, time-poor society, afflicted with information overload. Poetry can, in contrast, be almost profligate in its use of white space and silence.

Poems and prayers, and liturgical language in general, often make use of patterns, repetitions and refrains. Arguably some poems read like litanies, making repeated use of verbal formulas, building up a sense of mystery by an accumulation of images. Thus a poem may be written with a recurring refrain, just as church intercessions can comprise extemporised phrases and subject matter linked together with more formal responses. These can serve to set up reflective ways of reading, as words and images spiral back on themselves, encouraging deeper thought and further connections in the mind of the reader. Louis MacNeice's 'Prayer before Birth' uses this loose liturgical structure: 'I am not yet born: O hear me'. This can be a solemn sort of writing but it doesn't have to be. Take Christopher Smart's celebrated eighteenth century section, from a larger poetic work, of anaphoric verse about his cat Geoffrey. Each line begins with the liturgically adapted 'For':

For I will consider my cat Jeoffrey
For he is the servant of the living God, duly and daily praising him,

Here the formula is rather an attractive one, and accumulates into a kind of exalted oddball affection for its feline subject. Smart's work in its entirety—*Jubilate Agno*—is something altogether more complex and visionary but this particular fragment is a model for several contemporary poets from Wendy Cope to Deryn Rees-Jones. The form has the capacity to contain both humour and the beholding of the subject (a cat, a lover, a father) though accumulation of detail: liturgical response used to convey and explore human emotion.

Poetry can even mimic the monastic canonical hours (Lauds, Prime, etc)—Auden's later poems did, as do (rather less reverently) some of Thomas Merton's and Merton was a monk himself. Merton wrote his beautiful prose-poem sequence 'Hagia Sophia' when processing the spiritual but also very human, personal love he felt for the young nurse 'M'. The sections are structured by the rhythm of his monastic life; shot through with an extra light to that of merely physical longing. Here is an extract from 'High Morning: The Hour of Tierce':

> She is in all things like the air receiving the sunlight In her
> they prosper. In her they glorify God. In her they rejoice
> to reflect Him. In her they are united with him. She is the
> union between them.

Poetic-monastic vocations aside, we shouldn't be surprised at the blend of human and divine love which seems to find a prominence in poetry. The tradition goes back a long way to the Biblical 'Song of Songs', a lyrical account in startling imagery and fragmented voices of erotic and/or spiritual desire. True, the tradition is predominantly male-authored, but not exclusively so: the thirteenth century mystic Hadewijch of Brabant, for example, wrote beautiful poetry echoing the tradition of courtly love (noble knight devoted to unattainable lady), but for the Divine, with gender roles reversed. The first sonneteers took the tradition of human/divine love further—Petrarch for Laura, Dante for Beatrice—expressing love for a woman and through it accessed the language and imagery of spirituality too.

Formal poetry can be a lucid way of exploring spirituality. As in set prayers, the formula is there, and skill and concentration needed to keep language and imagery both technically accomplished and fresh. The sonnet especially has the double tradition of being a vehicle for love poetry and also for the philosophical, the ineffable, the spiritual. Its shape is universal—the 'small square box' as Don Paterson describes it—a mandala-like shape of words, crafted to draw the eye, to fit into the heart and allow a shift or deepening of insight. Carol Anne Duffy's 'Prayer' is a striking contemporary example of the form, speaking from the lonely dislocation of modern society: 'Sometimes, although we cannot pray, a prayer / Utters itself...' Duffy has written some highly accessible poetry based on biblical or religious themes but 'Prayer' arguably addresses the lack and loss which precede and promote language: 'the minims sung by a tree...the distant Latin chanting of a train'. The tone is elegiac, reminiscent of the lost security of childhood, perhaps of the first discrete elements of language learned: 'Inside, the radio's prayer –/ Rockall. Malin. Dogger. Finisterre.' The strong trochaic meter of this line sounds like an incantation, a prayer in itself. And here we can consider the 'alternative' life of poetry and spirituality, one that does not explain itself *in* words so much as point to the mystery beyond them. Duffy's last line hovers in space between the pre-linguistic and the semantic power of words and this is a very interesting area for the exploration of spirituality in poetry.

In 1911, at the height of the early modernist period's interest in mysticism, spirituality and psychology, Rudolph Otto published *The Idea of the Holy*. He suggests that it is the underlying rhythms and sounds of speech, rather than the grammatical meaning, which can convey the elusive wisdom of spirituality, as far as we can articulate this wisdom in language at all:

> The numinous [Otto's preferred term for a sense of spiritual presence] finds its most unqualified expression in the spell exercised by the only half intelligible language of devotion, and in the unquestionably real enhancement of the awe of the worshipper which this produces...

Otto was writing at a time when such ideas were influencing literature as much as, if not more than, religious thought but to some extent such ideas have always been present. One of the routes of mystical texts, of written attempts to convey the ineffable, has been to stretch language and push it beyond the grammatically coherent by using a wealth of contradictory, fragmentary phrases. This exemplifies the application of apophatic or 'negative' spirituality, a way of thinking about the divine which pushes us beyond what we think we know by letting the gaps and inadequacies of language play against insight and certainty. Julian of Norwich, the fourteenth century English mystic (and first woman to write a book in English) cheerfully describes God as 'mother, father and spouse' in the same sentence. She also tells of being led on impossible journeys (the wounded body, the deep sea, the past and future, the city within the soul) with equal aplomb, claiming her status as a visionary in order to speak, or write, with illogical, rhythmical clarity, of what she experiences.

For poetry, the idea of language going beyond its own ostensible meaning has obvious relevance. Particularly perhaps for the abstract lyricism of contemporary poetry, generally of the avant garde variety, which seeks in its use of language to lift the reader above a prescriptive interpretation, and to loosen the semantic associations of words and phrases enough to allow other insights to emerge. It may not be the case that 'communion with God' was the intention of the author but the text is often open to such a reading. Barbara Guest, Kathleen Fraser, Lisa Samuels, many others—a considerable list of writers who create a textual space for potential engagement with the divine. This is not, of course, to declare that all L=A=N=G=U=A=G=E poets or those influenced by such movements are writing texts for spiritual contemplation. But I would dare to argue that with some writers and poets the connection is there and is perhaps a connection more open to the numinous than the carefully crafted texts of self-declared contemporary religious poets. Here, for example, is a quotation from a poem by Kathleen Fraser:

forward edge itself to be volume by necessity as if partial erase
edge itself to be volume by necessity as if partial erase   other
itself to be volume by necessity as if partial erase   corners
to be volume by necessity as if partial erase   planes
volume by necessity as if partial erase   accumulate
by necessity as if partial erase   depth
necessity as if partial erase   condensed
as if partial erase   in
if partial erase   preparation
erase   stagework
of   historic
pearly   tendons
lucent   elaborate
decision   ribcage

from *Wing*, 'X. Vanishing Point: Third Black Quartet'

Fraser's writing is full of wings and flight. Certainly not a unique image cluster and one that has a sense of escape and vanishing as well as of spiritual aspiration. Here the text on the page presents a frame of white wing; as if the space enclosed by the repeating words is the real import of Fraser's writing. The use of the white space has a concrete quality, echoing back to Herbert's 'Easter Wings', itself a well-loved, religious piece. But I like very much the way the language empties itself, by a graceful process of erasure, into the 'lucent' absence of its central premise. Such a way of writing is certainly not the province of female poets only—rather the opposite, if anything. But I find it fascinating that feminist theorists in particular have embraced the idea of non-linear, open, fragmentary texts as a way of articulating experience which is arguably neither perceptible nor expressible in more closed language. Julia Kristeva, for example, engages creatively with mysticism, poetry, and the acquisition of language.

What of the links between poetry and 'impossible' visionary experience itself: can this also be an essential connection in reading poetry differently? Lisa Samuels has in fact written a poem about Julian of Norwich, as have several other twentieth century writers from T S Eliot onwards. Denise Levertov, Kathleen Jamie, Gillian Allnutt have all felt the pull of this medieval mystic and visionary. People sometimes talk loosely of the 'creative vision' of the writer and artist: meaning their sense of individual theme or subject set within a wider project, a consistent set of themes, an individual style. But some visions recorded by poetry, even contemporary poetry, are surprisingly and literally just that. I'm thinking particularly of Brendan Kennelly's sequence 'The Man Made of Rain'. Kennelly writes that in 1996 he had major heart surgery, a quadruple bypass. The day after the operation he had a number of visions. He saw a man made of rain. 'He spoke to me and took me on journeys', Kennelly writes. 'He led me to different places…such as the place where scars are roads through difficult territories…he took me into brilliant confusions to experience thrilling definitions, or moments of definition. He taught me the meaning of presence.' Kennelly wrote remarkable poems about these visions. The mysterious raining man is mentor, guardian angel, poetic symbol, inner self, the ultimate familiar stranger.

I looked into his crying eyes, how can
the rain be crying?
It is. Rain sheds itself, sheds tears as well,

the tears are running down his face
yet do not fall to earth.

This helps me to talk, he said.

Kennelly's long sequence explores the edges of existence and perception: it evokes a physical flooding and flowing which is somehow contained and become healing. Similar in many ways to the visions of the mystics, to those of Julian in particular, with her lucid recollection of surreal visions received *in extremis*. 'What is vision?' asks Kennelly in his preface. 'It is completely normal when you're going through it, odd or tricky when you try to speak of it afterwards...Vision, when experienced, is normal as rain falling on trees, grass, gravel, flowers, streets, people. Vision waits for us, ready to give itself.' And it is left to the reader of such texts to make a leap to the impossible, and to trust that truth can reveal itself in inexplicable ways: very much the aim of *Lectio Divina*. When a sense of mystery is present and communicates itself, 'gives' itself, then the reader has discovered the core of both spirituality and poetry.

A final paradox to end this essay: both poetry and mystical prayer not only include but point towards silence. Poetry is the nearest written form we have to silence, with its spare use of language, its generous incorporation of space and 'white' page. Mystical prayer is also spare in its use of language; short mantras serve better to promote silence than lengthy theological paragraphs, as the author of the fourteenth century 'Cloud of Unknowing' points out. Poems which can make the reader stop and taste silence are perhaps the best poems of all, and often include a deeply felt, even though lightly worn spirituality. Jane Hirschfield does this wonderfully. There is, for example, a moment of sudden insight in her 'A Breakable Spell' where language shows itself to be both elusive and liable to slip into vision and silence. A word is on the tip of the poet's tongue, 'trying *window* / trying *egret*', and suddenly the egret manifests itself into a glimpse of visual unity that becomes— literally reflects—a vision of silence:

she stands with her
elegant legs
black in the water.
Below her, another looks up.

My love,
there is no sound between them.

This is beautiful writing, savouring silence as a gift. Elizabeth Jennings, in *Every Changing Shape,* her book on poetry and mysticism, refers to a 'combination of intense peace with intense concentration' when describing the essence of both poetry and prayer. This at least seems to be the best way of reading poetry as a textual place for spiritual insight. The concentration is one of willing belief (or at least suspension of disbelief). The peace is a leap of silence, from page to reader, reader to their God (or however we wish to describe our source of creativity), and back again.

September 2005

Notes

[1] *On First Principles,* quoted in Jantzen, *Power, Gender and Christian Mysticism* (Cambridge: CUP, 1995), 69.

Bibliography

Duffy, Carol Ann, 'Prayer' in *Mean Time,* London: Anvil Press Poetry, 1993
Fraser, Kathleen, Selection of work in *Out of Everywhere, Linguistically Innovative Poetry by Women in North America & the UK,* ed. O'Sullivan, London: Reality Street Editions, 1996.
Hirschfield, Jane,'A Breakable Spell' in *Each Happiness Ringed by Lions, Selected Poems,* Newcastle: Bloodaxe Books, 2005
James, William, *The Varieties of Religious Experience,* Harmondsworth: Penguin Books, 1983 (1902)

Jantzen, Grace, *Power, Gender and Christian Mysticism*, Cambridge: Cambridge University Press, 1995

Jennings, Elizabeth, *Every Changing Shape: Mystical Experience and the Making of Poems*, Manchester: Carcanet Press, 1996 (1961)

Kennelly, Brendan, 'The Man Made of Rain' (1998) in *Familiar Strangers: New and Selected Poems 1960–2004*, Newcastle: Bloodaxe Books, 2004

Merton, Thomas, 'Hagia Sophia', in *In the Dark Before Dawn, New Selected Poems*, New York: New Directions, 2005.

Otto, Rudolph, *The Idea of the Holy*, Harmondsworth: Penguin Books, 1959 (1911)

Paterson, Don (ed.), *101 Sonnets from Shakespeare to Heaney*, London: Faber, 1999

Underhill, Evelyn, *Mysticism*, London: One World, 1993 (1911).

Almost Unreadable:
Contemporary Elegists and The Poetics of Metaphysical and Emotional Limit

PETER MIDDLETON

Modern elegies are difficult to read. Not because they offer obscure references, cryptic parataxes, puzzlingly rapid transitions of theme, or language games whose rules are almost indecipherable (although there are a few that do); this is an altogether more existential difficulty, a barrier to understanding that is rarely due only to verbal or conceptual complexity. Elegies stir emotions, memories, biographical questions, and metaphysical speculations, whose turbulence can overwhelm interpretive clarity and yet whose relevance cannot be dismissed as mere sentimental or idiosyncratic distraction. Most accounts of elegy therefore understandably sidestep this problem by concentrating on issues that can be dealt with more objectively, whether issues of the psychology or ethnography of mourning, or the changing historical forms of the elegy's public or civic role. A few commentators even deny that the modern elegy exists at all. I think if we don't rush to shrug off the uneasiness and confusion generated by these poems, but think of it as an acute form of a much more general feature of contemporary poetry, the modern elegy can point us to a more accurate critical discourse.

When an older friend was discovered floating dead in a reservoir outside the city where he lived, I tried several times to write a poem in his memory. None of the poems worked until I wrote a very different poem about his many often angry attempts to mentor me, not least as a writer, to guide my steps and reading in ways which he often wished had been his, and my poem lined itself with a retrospective anger as well as the sense of loss and guilt at not having supported him in hard times. Even this poem felt threadbare and stained with bad faith. I don't want to treat my poetry as a wall on which to pin up images and memories of those who have fallen, as if like a lost pet, the friend might be found by the right reader, and walk in one day with the water streaming off him as he chants the redeeming syllables of the elegy.

A justifiable elegy would seem to be one in which the working through of language and its scenes of conflict between exploitation and ethical resistance, might necessitate the ritual placement of the dead within its naming, thinking and feeling. But this necessity is what is hard to articulate or justify, especially when contemporary poetry is permeated by a low hum of elegiac memory in the personal lyric, and in the culture at large governments increasingly seize on the political opportunities of collective, media-driven mourning to win mass support for their military adventures. Elegies are ways of forgetting as well as honoring memory. They ought to help the living untangle the debts attached to the dead, and redirect the love and fury once elicited by the dead towards the poesis of a new society. But this is not a manual for future elegies or a draft contract for the negotiations between writers and readers. I want to puzzle over three elegies which fascinate and faze me, and to start with the most obvious cause, an imbalance of ignorance or inside knowledge between text and reader that is felt more than reasoned.

David Antin: 'definitions for mendy'

David Antin's elegy, 'definitions for mendy' (the title is entirely in lower case) was first published in book form in *definitions* (Caterpillar, 1967), alongside two other poems, 'trip through a landscape' and 'the black plague/ parts I–IV.' Anyone who has only read the poem in Antin's *Collected Poems* or in Eliot Weinberger's anthology, *American Poetry Since 1950*, will have missed this dimension of the poem. At first glance the book designed by the poet's wife, the artist Eleanor Antin, doesn't look like a book at all; it is spiral bound, has cheap brown cardboard covers, and pages printed with the blue squares used for elementary arithmetic and writing exercises. It looks like a school exercise book on which someone has written the word 'definitions' in lower case (perhaps for an English class), and the name David Antin beneath. The cover also has lines headed 'Name' and 'Address', and their capitalisation makes them seem more authoritative than the title and the name of the author. in what looks like a school exercise book. Here an owner/reader of the book can assert their property rights. Already I am puzzled even before I have begun reading. Why this format? The effect is not only to place the poem in a context that irresistibly insists on childhood and early schooling: it also, more disturbingly, makes any reader feel that they too are suddenly infantilised, or at least, sent back to school.

But it is Mendy who becomes the conscious locus of my need for interpretive help. Who is he, what did he mean to the author, and why does this seem to matter? Another way of explaining the difficulty is that if I knew that Mendy the friend is a fiction, that the man in the 'orange jacket and workpants and a blue denim shirt' never existed, or even if he did, never said that it felt 'queer' to be dying, then I would read the poem differently. Everything about the poem encourages the reader not to read it as masochistic fantasy, and to trust the honesty of the details of its grief. The difficulty is that my relation to it as a specific reader at a distance from any intimacy with the poet or inside knowledge of his life (and perhaps my lack of scholarship too) that might provide a clear refutation of any such lingering doubts about authenticity, sets up an initial disturbance whose vortex then draws in other observations and responses.

The poem is highly performative. It is very much an act of mourning in the sense that the structure insists on the lines as markers of a temporal series of discrete and carefully measured assertions (not an atemporal moment or sequence of equivalent propositions that therefore pre-empt duration), that also mark currents of feeling. Pedantry, repetition, images in decay, as well as the increasing pathos of the attempt to find solace in the expected clarities of scientific definitions and the reasoning they entail, all incur emotional expenditure on the part of a reader, and possibly some forensic questioning of the process taken by the poet's reactions. The surface of expression is unusually dispassionate for an elegy, which makes it immediately compelling to search for any faultlines through which passions might be escaping. As each of a set of materialist terms like loss, value, body, weight, duration are defined and tested, they are found to leak inarticulate feelings. Longing for the impossible, to see Mendy again, is compared to other basic instincts, hunger and thirst, which then leads into a meditation on what would satisfy those longings, bread and water. These become signs of the friend's absence—'a glass of water is between us'. An extended chain of similar states and signs of absence create an impression of a continuous line of reasoning, whose termination in a surreal set of images is even more shocking: the poem conjures up the dead man whose initially ordinary appearance belied by 'a blue crab' biting his hand, a face like a clock with both a salamander motif and a dial fluorescent with radium, a floor on fire, and an image of the desert mysteriously superimposed on his mouth. The anti-realism of this dream-like figure is both a visual equivalent for the phenomenology of bereavement and an involuntary dialectical image of the materialist consolation.

Physics appears to be ready to provide the answer to Mendy's fall from life

> a glass of water falling
> is a falling body of water
> and obeys the laws of falling bodies
> according to which
> all bodies fall
> [...]
> at the level of the sea
> the earth pulls all bodies down

And the poem drily comments in the next line—'the thirst is not appeased.' It is not so much that the mourner has misapplied the metaphoric potential of the physics of gravity, as that the physics has borrowed some of its rhetorical force from the condition of mortality. Where an earlier poet would have found his or her state of bereavement mirrored in the natural world or the meterology, the contemporary poet finds it in the scientific world-picture, but since a direct projection would simply suggest a highly pathetic fallacy, the poem circumnavigates this risk by trusting to the scientific discourse to help. Again and again the poem smashes into the limits of science: 'the glass of water slips to the floor'. It tries to imagine the permanence of Mendy's death by meditating on the idea of 'duration' and trying to find predicates for this temporal abstraction made so painful by his death, only to give it up as impossible. This name, 'duration', fails to name—'it does not mean anything/ it cannot tell time'—just as the name Mendy now fails to name an actual, existing being.

In its final three sections the poem tries out three forms of consolation. One is memory, a memory of Mendy telling the poet what it felt like to be dying; one is a short lyrical section of traditional elegiac comfort in the cyclical renewal of the natural world, a text laid out in the style of William Carlos Williams, evoking the contrast of flowering forsythia alongside a stretch of 'black water'; and the final section which then combines these two strategies with the scientific discourse and finds an ascetic consolation in the observation that 'the eye cannot discriminate true intensities of light/ only their ratio,' and nor can the ear hear pure tones, only differences. Loss of Mendy brings with it a truer sense of who Mendy was and is, because his absence creates such contrasts of silence and conversation, appearance and invisibility. But this is a harsh doctrine and the slow movement of the varying length end-stopped lines evokes a heavy melancholy that cannot be fully countered by the renewing intellectual energy of enquiry that turns to the scientific language.

What makes the poem difficult to read is not only the strange material format that implies youthful ignorance waiting for enlightenment that does not fully materialise, and the thematic dominance of seemingly irrelevantly abstract meditations on scientific terms. It is the way the poem empties out all the descriptive terms, the nouns especially, that arrive confident in their power to name, and then leave unable to 'mean anything,' that causes readerly confusion. Mendy is not the only name that doesn't stand up to a reader's need for definition: nouns in this poem have a half-life like radium, and produce darkness more than light. Dissonant tones range from the aphasic to the reasonable and to lyric passion. Scientific language appears to be a language of mourning, and like a suspect in a murder enquiry, doesn't seem to be grieving enough, as if perhaps it played a larger part in his demise than its avowed innocence would claim. Elegy expands to include the entire material universe, and contracts to the vanishing point of meaning.

Alice Notley: 'How We Spent the Last Year of His Life'
These are not quite elegies. They shade into the autobiography of a poet that unfolds across the 69 poems of Alice Notley's collection, *Mysteries of Small Houses* (Penguin, 1998), a trade paperback with a stylish green and orange colour, and endorsements that predictably chrome it with adjectives ('major', 'inexorable', 'wild', 'post-modern shamanism'). Elegy is not quite bounded enough to be generically interpretable, and this time my puzzlement is reinforced by an excess of personal entanglement. I can't read it without seeing Alice Notley herself,

recalling my only glimpse of Ted Berrigan and the dismissive comments of another poet, and above all, Douglas Oliver, Notley's husband after Berrigan, who himself died just two years after this volume appeared. I can't decide whether I read the accounts of loss and poverty in the poems as foreshadowing the death of Oliver, whom I knew well enough to grieve for, or as variants on an unstated mourning for him. And this intrusive response won't be argued out of the way, or repressed as displaced narcissism. To do so would be to fail to meet the poems' call for emotional honesty and commitment to the poetry.

Notley has developed a subtle style here that appears to be at once artlessly conversational and yet choreographed into the most complex syntaxes that register the fluctuations of recall, its sharpness, wonder, retaliation, and fear. Elegy arrives when she remembers how she and Berrigan were living with the knowledge of his illness in the small flat in New York, and might have anticipated his death:

> In our apartment we have imagined
> a world which abuses much less
> and imagined his encroaching death
> or did we forget to imagine that, did we
> imagine our affection only, "our best work"? (69)

Poetry stands for the relationship's love, as it comes to stand as the justification of this life, as its measure and loss (The title of the poem 'Gladly Though I Lost It and Knew I Would' is also the final line, where the words not only exemplify the tenderness that they created mutually, but also the power of poetry to manifest and memorialise it, hatched by the addition of commas to the clause: 'gladly, though I lost it, and knew I would.') Always she is aware of the intermittence of retrospective clarity. 'I can't get at the poem of this'(65) follows the admission that despite her pride that she and Ted had managed to live on very little money, 'the only thing that suffered was Ted's/ Health it suffered considerably'. Absence of the full-stop is a defiance of the judgemental logic that would masquerade as a two-sentence cause-and-effect, and its absence is also the point at which the poem is reading off the emotional temperature, the rage, the guilt, the bravado, and the pain of such admissions as this: 'I'm being self-righteous so / I can own my own past again.'(66)

As Berrigan's death approaches in the sequence, the poetry flinches. 'How We Spent the Last Year of His Life' begins with the observation of a temporal pattern that seems to restore Berrigan to an earlier emotional source: 'Ted's mother Peggy dies in July and Ted dies the following July.'(70) The connection between them had been made by Notley years before. In 'Poem' from *Waltzing Matilda* (Kulchur, 1981), Notley had written: 'Lively Peg / He married me, we say, because I smile like her.' (34) The flatness of the line about the two related deaths is followed by a momentary withdrawal of memory's permissions to travel back, as the poem is brought up short in the present of its writing:

> Ted's mother Peggy dies in July and Ted dies the following July
> the year between a painful mess; it's raining as usual in Paris
> who would want to talk of this and if I don't the book's
> > diminished
> in its exploration of a self, I'm speaking of a dying person
> embedded in certain ways self to self with me: how will we
> extricate each other, to exist as separate essences? (70)

This is the question that the elegising returns to repeatedly in asides and in its explicit preoccupations with the risk of the poetry being a failure. This risk is vindicated by the very material form of the commercial book, a success when measured against the many years of small press publication and no fame. In this poem, just two lines after this passage, ellipses are followed by the present-moment reflection—'This poem is prosaic'—and a few lines later, after a cliché has been left uncut, the poem laments again—'oh prosaic still'—and even after a poignant memory of her wilful blindness towards Berrigan's rapid deterioration, it comments—'No, that sounds like prose.' Prose represents not just the quotidian, it also suggests the aversion to risk that makes everyday life possible ('watch your step / (prose not poetry).' If there were any poetry to be found in this material, it would be 'beneath the prose / of whose bad behaviour ours or theirs.' 'Point of Fidelity' actually presents a short section with the title 'Poem' (a title that Notley has often used as if readerly doubt would add further wax to the surface) and it recounts a ritual associated in her mind and Berrigan's with Egypt, in which she invokes Osiris.

The poems about Berrigan's death concentrate on the shock it induces, a sense of 'blackness inside unmechanical / a sort of / breath / that isn't always / breathed.' Her difficulty with breathing is recognised by the linebreaks as an involuntary mimesis of Berrigan's own death, of mortality, that 'breath that isn't always.'(73) The next poem, 'Point of Fidelity' uses extensive repetition, of the act of carrying a sanitary towel upstairs and then swallowing a Valium tablet in the shape of a heart. Once again, the act of writing the poem is made to stand for the process of mourning:

> There's catastrophe, a poem
> "I keep seeing all those bodies"
> Wrench back from a fiction
> The bodies are really there then
> Catastrophe is in the real poem (75)

This in turn leads on to poems about mourning, in which she first claims that it is not a cultural construction ('grief is visible, substantial, I've literally seen it') and then compares it to possession by a god. Separation is terribly hard, because: 'If the other who dies is partly me, / and that me dies and another grows, the medium it grows in is grief.'(78)

My reading of the poems is at its most intense in 'I-Towards a Definition,' where it is not so much the tension between the apparent naivety of unpunctuated oral syntax ('I know I didn't make it what made it') and the resonance of ambiguities ('I didn't make it' = I didn't invent it, project it from my mind or I was defeated, killed), although that is emotionally buffeting enough. It's the exposure of pain, overstatement, revelation, dogmatic assertion indicating possession by intransigent feelings, all of which in ordinary converse invite responsive intimacies and disclosures, which here take the form of all the extras that I pour into the mix from my own relations with poet and poetry. I think that Notley's sequence is a challenge to reflect passionately on this.

Ric Caddel: *For the Fallen*
For the Fallen (Pig Press, 1997), was published in an edition of 21 copies (although mine says in red biro that it is 'ex-series' which implies more

were printed) as a photocopied, stapled pamphlet. It has the same yellow covers used for an entire series of Pig Press publications, whose name, 'Staple Diet' (drawing attention through its low-intensity pun to the low-budget, high-speed production as well as the claim to a sustaining poetics) is printed in a much larger font than the book's title peering out of a cutaway window. A note at the back provides a context for reading the poem:

> *For the Fallen* is a reading of Aneirin's *Y Gododdin*, and is taken from A.O.H.Jarman's edition (1988). It is done in memory of my son Tom. The three sections reflect, roughly, three methods of "translation": 1–39 selective literal translation; 40–75 loose phonic translation; 76–100 free palimpsest rendering. It is unlikely that any of these approaches would satisfy a scholar of Old Welsh.

From another scholar of this recondite material, Kenneth Hurlstone Jackson I learn that the Welsh poem is a sequence of elegies for the soldiers of a small army of men from Gododdin (called Wotadini by the Romans), a kingdom in what is now Southern Scotland, who were wiped out all but one or two men, in a battle with the Angles in Northumbria around the year 600, one the most forgotten periods of history over the past two and half millenia. One comment by Jackson seems particularly pertinent: 'the whole tone is contemporary, not harking back to a distant past; the poet is praising and lamenting his own relatives and friends, people he knew well, whose character he describes with a personal knowledge which was no doubt shared by his listeners and was intended to appeal to them as such.'(56) Jackson is trying to defend his conclusion that the poem is not a fiction, that this is a sequence of genuine elegies written at the time of the battle by a friend of the fallen, rather than what he calls 'bogus eulogistic bardic poems'(58), but it equally describes Caddel's reworking.

By now it may seem that I am primarily attributing the difficulty of the modern elegy to the irreducibly involving authenticity that coevality brings. But when I read Caddel's poem sequence I cannot help thinking of the terse letter he sent when his son was killed by falling down a stairwell, to say that he would have to hand over the final business of the anthology we were editing for *Talisman*. Imagination baulks at the loss of a friend's child, a loss so terrible that any commentary would seem to risk insensitivity and one's own emotions, perhaps especially if one is also a parent, would be likely to add another line of affective instrumentation to an already highly wrought text. I don't think this is the whole story, however. I shall suggest that Caddel's poems make more apparent what most contemporary poetry also does in varying intensities contingent on intimacy and knowledge, and that Caddel shows exceptional tact in avoiding any special pleading for the poetry on the basis of experience (compare many contemporary poets, Sharon Olds for instance). What is remarkable about this great poem is the degree to which it doesn't presume on its testimony.

One of the most powerful lyrics in Caddel's sequence is no.45, which is a partially homophonic rendering of *Canu Aneirin* xliii.A.

I'm droning dreary and dry	*Am drynni drylaw drylenn*
I'm loose and I'm this-ways walking	*am lwys amdiffwys dywarchen.*
I'm widow-wilt in your head	*am gwydaw gwallt e ar benn.*
I am wire eagle with them	*y am wyr eryr gwydyen.*
with news along the way then	*gwyduc neus amuc ae waiw*
dulled duelled and broken	*ardullyat diwyllyat e berchen.*
amid more yen	*amuc moryen*
when was Merlin a courteous pen	*gwenwawt mirdyn. a chyvrannv penn*
price in words was a shallow shamen	*prif eg weryt. ac an nerth ac am hen;*
try where a big gun was brandished	*trywyr yr bod bun bratwen.*
during when and why my son went	*deudec gwenabwy vab gwenn.*

Caddel's version takes a lament for (in Jackson's translation) 'the men of the Eagle, Gwydden the fierce,' Morien who buried the chief's head, the warrior Bradwen, and 'Gwenabwy son of Gwen' (133) and transforms it into something very different, retaining the military references as metaphors of a personal condition. Maybe it is wrong to call them metaphors, because this is a history that is a part of a distant historical horizon in Northumberland where Caddel lives. His verse is meta-poetic enough to be aware of the implications of such archeological bardolatry. He describes the poem's tone and structure with a knowing irony that shifts into a harsh judgement on poet and poetry implied by the submerged rhetorical question about that precognitive shaman, Merlin, who may or may not be one of the 'shallow shamen.' 'Shamen' is as overdetermined as any word in the poem, shivering with shame, shamed men, and charm, at the very least.

Extreme instability troubles the language throughout. To transmute 'bod bun' into 'big gun' is to treat the Welsh as a severe distortion, as if the language were now just a distant incomprehensible rumble of sounds, and yet perhaps it is at least half reasonable, since 'bun' which means a spearhead might be equated in modern terms with a gun, even if the word 'bod' is a form of the verb 'to be' rather than an adjective. This is a poem where distortion of meaning, language and word order is the central device for representing the metamorphoses of grief.

The final section of *For the Fallen* can be terrifying in its rage, its sense of ruined or abandoned lyric forms, its sudden swerves from reflective musing to 'calamity discourse red and away.' Merlin reappears in a haiku missing a syllable: 'trawl Merlin by sea/ three strands of white flowers/ blow on the world's bards.' White flowers of grief may be a blow against poetry or may strew themselves on the poets like a blessing, or is this wishful interpretation? The poem constantly challenges the reader to weigh such consolations against fatality.

In the final poems *Y Gododdin* is fading back into the Dark Ages about which historians know so little, and echoes from Housman, Shakespeare, or Donne, as in the following poem, are more evident:

gaily over the mosslawn
into this fairness //
go with ragwort and cinquefoil
tapping our Eden for free
meant for a gaffer at law
       chance kings and desperate men
caring cathedral by // grey play at
       womble muck and sneedball
if only my boy had been a bear
       him roughly treated
// upon earths green mantle
       death be not proud

The poem alludes to the wonderful line from Russell Hoban's book *How Tom Beat Captain Najork and His Hired Sportsmen* (Jonathan Cape, 1974) when Captain Najork says, 'Right...We shall play womble, muck, and sneedball, in that order.' Captain Najork has been brought in by Tom's nasty aunt in order to teach him a lesson, that he should stop fooling around. Tom is alone. To his reasonable inquiry as to who will be on his side, Captain Najork just replies, 'nobody.' Tom, however, wins the battle with the Captain, because he is better at all the skills needed for these special games than the adult champions, and a role reversal takes place: 'Captain Najork broke down and wept.' Tom takes the Captain's boat and goes off to find a new aunt and start a new life. Intertextuality becomes intensely elegiac here as the convergence of names, fates, and emotions induce endless looping.

The repeated use of a double backslash acts not just as punctuation, and echo of packet signal protocol, but as sigils for the falling man, and doing so they jolt perception away from the cognitive act of reading printed words for meaning to the muteness of emblem. Silence and absence. The first section offers poems of a few lines often only one word long, as if most of the other words from the Welsh poem had no relevance any more, and what remains are the only words that can still be heard and at least partially understood:

36
never
great
fiery
he would not make
fame
resounded
rock of
son of

Words are more freely used though, more crowded in the second and third sections, but the use of the original text and its literal translation as signs of loss measured by the distance from Caddel's text continues throughout. As a whole the sequence shares with the original the sense of a grief so strong that its expression has to be repeated over and over for relief.

Experimentalism reads here as instability, incompletion, and endlessness of thought troubled by the awful truths of death and irredeemability. Yet this might make the poem sound leaden or tricky, when it is everywhere deft, swift in thought, and above all works with great tact across the histories of fallen men. Reading it is immersive, and emotionally exhausting, or rather emotionally challenging. I can think of few contemporary poetic texts that ask us to think so hard about our commitments to reading and writing, to the values of life and politics we bring to it.

Afterthoughts

Elegies such as these do a lot of cultural work. All of them are working to forget with care. Antin wants Mendy's loss to become valuable insight. Notley is a chronicler, choosing what to remember for the literary world, what to lose. Caddel is the closest to the maelstrom of not making it, and his entire poem presses hard on what can be remembered and what has been or must be forgotten with unbearable care. Elegies? Tar babies, irresistibly passionate appeals for reparation that can never happen, teasing metaphysics, memento mori, fine poems. I haven't an epigram or rounded paragraph of summary. The implications of these poems still trouble me, and I don't want to rehearse the various theories of elegy, mourning and melancholy that readers will surely have met already. Rather I want to thank these poets, and to add that their poems should remind us that our reflections on poetics in these times of a new politics of televisually grief-stricken rage ought to take account of the entangled banks of personal history and public culture that are so evident in the encounters that I have narrated here. And emotion? Feelings are as much a part of words as sound, rhythm, etymology, and the traces of bardic elegy from the far off beginnings of Welsh poetry. I can't say more.

from The Middle Room

Jennifer Moxley

Author's Note. Occasions for elegy are not always appropriately solemn. Sometimes they are too unbelievable. A tangible feeling of *absence* can arise not only from the loss of something once held, but also from the loss of something one never had in the first place. Such is the absence of a lost possibility—something or someone *truly lost* that neither hope nor wishing can bring back.

The following excerpt comes from the second chapter of *The Middle Room*, a book about a unique group of people I met at the University of California at San Diego, and how my encounter with them in many ways set the tone, if not the course, for my life in poetry. Naturally my relationship to my family, with which the following is primarily concerned, also comes into it. As this is an *excerpt*, taken *in medias res*, some references and names are not fully explained, but these do not, I think, hamper reading or obscure the central episode.

"I Can't Take Any More Guy Lombardo"

In an effort to establish more succinctly my 'state of mind' when, about half-way through the semester, Chuck proposed that he and I temporarily 'swap cars', my '68 Mustang for his '79 Toyota Celica, I must now relate, as if I were a lawyer using extenuating circumstances to explain the irrational acts of my client, the sad tale of my life as a car owner, the unfolding of which resembles to an astonishing degree, if we are to believe the fictional narratives, the story of a hero's first love, the memory of whom, usually concentrated in a physical attribute, such as a curve of lip (as was Man Ray's misfortune with Lee Miller), or a cascade of dark ringlets down the back of an exposed neck, gently manacles him to a counterfeit existence, an endless search for the woman who can understudy his lost Aphrodite and who, god forbid he should find her, will suffer for her reality a violent resentment the origin of which she may never know.

Born in a city of freeways, for as long as I could remember cars had been as much a part of my life as eating, showering, or going to sleep when I felt myself to be tired, a dependence based on geographical happenstance that I never resented but rather, as a Parisian loves the Métro because, if for no other reason, he cannot imagine his world without it, I loved cars, not as a connoisseur loves them, fetishizing certain expensive makes or rare models, but rather as a child loves their matchbox counterparts, enchanted by the ability they have, as he guides them along the kitchen floor past obstacles—cat dish, cereal box, napkin ring—that he himself has placed there, making the engine sounds with his mouth, to fuel and energize his imagination.

If I leave aside my childhood fascination with 'Lolly', my family's Volkswagen camper van, whose tiny built-in ice box and pump sink provided me, more devastatingly than any doll house had ever done, with numerous domestic fantasies and thoughts of 'self reliance', then the first time my general love became specific was a few months shy of my seventeenth birthday when, one sunny morning, I walked out of the Albatross Street house and was struck by a vision as glorious as Beatrice must have been to Dante when he found her attendant and divine in the third and final section of his *Commedia*: there, in the raised cement driveway of the house just opposite, sat, perched high upon the smallest of wheels, a darling red 1960 Chevrolet Corvair. As though it were a sparkling piece of tin foil and I a scavenging raven, I headed immediately towards this car, my beeline quickened by a flimsy paper 'For Sale' sign taped inside of the passenger's window. This sign produced in me, who minutes earlier had been content with borrowing my mother's car, the overwhelming anxiety of desire coupled with the nervous anticipation of a child who fears that, in the time it takes to run home and fetch the money from his secret hiding place, the one remaining pencil set in the window of the five-and-dime bearing the image of Captain Marvel will be bought up, most likely out of spite by his wealthy nemesis, and lost to him, who alone understands the deeper meaning of its value, for all eternity.

How desperately and how instantaneously I wanted that car! Now do not think that I was without resources, for I had abandoned my full-time schooling the year before and was just then gainfully employed as a clerk and stock person at my father's store, The Mexico Shop, a modest retail business that dealt in imported trinkets, piñatas, jewellery, pottery and the like, located in that part of the city called 'Old Town' which had

73

been landscaped to resemble *days of yore* with the tourist's disposition especially in mind. The problem was that at this part-time work I earned less than the minimum wage, and thus I figured that my accounts held but $200 ready cash to put towards the car, a meagre portion of the written asking price of $1,200. Undeterred by my insufficiency of funds I galloped back into the house, calling "Mom! Mom! Mom!" excitedly as I went. As when faced with the dilemma of my antique desk, I took her by the hand, led her outside and showed her the desired object, all the while explaining what an extraordinary thing it was that such an opportunity should present itself to *us,* especially now as, with my schedule more hectic than ever, the pressure on her car had increased and so on and what luck to have such a solution 'pop up' right under our noses.

Whether she viewed the acquisition of cars as falling under male jurisdiction, or was simply weary of my capitalist advertisements for the necessity of what were, in essence, *luxury items,* I do not know, but Jo, in an unprecedented move, declined to give me her aid and directly recommended that I ask my father, who was not prone to releasing monies unless the law required it of him, to extend me the loan in her stead. True, I was in his current employ and could therefore guarantee remuneration, if in nothing else then in hours of labor, but despite the convenient logic of this reasoning I still felt that with those three alien words, "ask your father," my mother had placed an impediment between me and my heart's desire as grand as the one the Wizard had when he demanded that Dorothy bring him the broomstick of the Wicked Witch of the West. I did not fear my father, a slow-gaited man who looked a bit as though he had great schooners tied to the bottoms of his feet when he walked and who, being extraordinarily near-sighted, owned four different pairs of thick horn-rimmed glasses, one for reading, one for walking, one for watching television and yet another for sports, but neither was I in the habit of asking him for help. Though not a cruel man, my father could nevertheless be very grave, appearing as he often did preoccupied with those sorts of thoughts—finance, insurance, the future of trade and so forth—that children, suspecting such ridiculous preoccupations strange ailments of the adult mind, spend many a sleepless hour, out of concern for their parents, vainly seeking to remedy.

Before submitting my petition to him, I went to the owners of the Corvair and asked that they 'hold' the car for me, assuring them that I was on the verge of acquiring the funds to buy it, a measure of security which was in the end totally superfluous, for, as it turned out, in yet another example of what I believed to be a 'universal desire' turning out to be quite singular to me, I alone showed interest in this old, outdated, and purportedly dangerous car. And what of my success with my father? What can I say without retrospectively casting, by virtue of his so-called greater authority and wisdom, a negative light upon my young and eager self? Without a shred of hesitation he turned me down flat on the grounds that I was not mature enough to handle the responsibility of paying back such a large sum! *And I could not convince him otherwise.* Though I did so within earshot of no one, I vowed at that moment never to ask him for anything again. I was horrified by the thought that if the innate honesty of my character was *all but invisible* to him whose very genetic stuff had gone into my making, then *who,* I thought, *who* is not barred from being able to see it? My mother, who never lacked for comment on her erstwhile husband's flaws, saw in my dilemma a perfect opportunity to indulge in a catalog of his paternal abuses and come to the rescue of her poor, abandoned, careless daughter. Adopting, with not a little pomp, the very arguments I had so recently made to her deaf ear, she loaned me the thousand dollars and the Corvair, which she immediately nicknamed 'little red', became my very own.

Having been built before the popularization of FM radio my Corvair received only AM, a modulation I had lately scorned on the grounds that it was 'for nerds', but that soon revolutionized my musical tastes as I began listening to 'the music of your life' on the big band station KMLO. I was accompanied on all my journeys—to friends' houses, to the movies, to and from work—by 'the music of your life', and out of my vague dissatisfaction with the contemporary world this big band sound began to form in me a protean nostalgia that, though sometimes spilling onto the battlefields, seemed mainly to anchor itself between the wars. The clarinet, the whiny brass, a high and clear female voice became, as had been great expanses of grass to my earlier equine fantasies, catalysts of a *sensuous longing*, which produced in me *nostalgic passions* such as the desire to wear seamed stockings and dance beneath the flickering lights of a mirrored chandelier. Questing after this desire I attended a few KMLO-sponsored evenings with my little brother Fred as escort. There among the cafeteria tables, lined up like battleships off the coast, Fred and I would sit and listen to the seventeen-piece big band, carrying in our 'old kit bag' some thirty years less experience than anyone else in the room. Couples hard-pressed to walk easily outdanced us and then, puffing heavily over plastic cups of punch, appended our already vivid imaginations, for both Clyde and my father were veterans, of World War II.

Never now was I not listening to 'so and so ... *and his orchestra*' as I wended my way to work through those neighborhoods my Corvair preferred for their gentle sloping hills and wide courtly streets flanked by palm trees and haciendas. As if nothing divisive had passed between me and my father, I continued to arrive at eight to sweep the tile sidewalk in front of his shop, the dust agitated by my push broom billowing up like dry face powder. After hanging the piñatas, I would spend the rest of the day in the basement, cool and peaceful, unpacking wooden crates filled with tangled strips of straw in which were nestled clay pots, pre-Colombian figurines, and hand-blown Mexican glass. I brought tapes of my music to listen to as I worked, which increasingly, as I recorded them from my new records, were compilations of my favorite swing bands.

One extraordinary afternoon, as the sirens with their beautiful song would have lured Odysseus, had he not been so cunning, to his death, the sound of Benny Goodman's clarinet lured my father in from off the dusty lot to the basement doorway. He stopped there with the sun at his back as if he were an old caballero just returned from a long, tiring ride, and though in the shadow I could not see his features he turned his head in my direction and said, in a weary and low-pitched voice, "I had no idea that you liked this music." *How could he have.* He from whom my very being was hidden behind a murky rampart of femininity, he who could not see that the very car he had judged me too puerile to sensibly captain was directly responsible for creating this strange convergence of events: the clarinet, the sun, my caballero father and myself, all for a moment frozen into a formal configuration the symbolism of which rivalled even the most fantastically rendered and frightening of those pre-Colombian figurines, presently lined up in a phalanx atop the work table, awaiting the strings of little white price tags to be tied around their arms. He walked into the room, sat down on a pigskin chair and, as a strange, dishevelled, and lonely man will tell you of a time in his life when he was envied and respected, my father told me that as a student he had, with a keen ear and a quick pen, been the much feared music reviewer of the University of Oregon weekly, and that in this capacity he had played a strong role in determining, at least among the college set, the making or breaking of the latest 78s.

The paper-thin spirit of a man sitting before me cast in the role of 'hepcat' eventually brought down by domestication evoked a history unlike any I had previously imagined for my father, he who had once been tied most strongly to the image of a plate of iced oatmeal cookies, his favorite after-dinner treat, and then retired to the couch where he finished every evening, or at least those I was fortunate enough to witness during one of my 'visits', bourbon and water sweating on the glass-top coffee table, assiduously watching the Easter-colored organza dresses and tuxedos of the hired dancers swinging to a canned version of 'Elmer's Tune' on the Lawrence Welk music hour. Many years after his basement confession I unearthed hard evidence of this earlier connoisseurship when I discovered, while cleaning out the garage of Albatross Street, in a locked, rusty, gray metal file cabinet, an enormous stack of love letters he had sent in courtship from Mazatlan to my mother in San Francisco. They were typed on airmail stationary with letterhead from the Hotel Playa, the paper aged now to a pale yellow, and in them he had adopted the phonetic spelling of words in imitation of his hero Ernest Hemingway. Bemoaning his inability to get a hold of good jazz records to accompany the mixing of his famous 'Martinis Moxley', my dad had written in one of his post scripts: "Send me down some Dave Brubeck Jo, *I can't take any more Guy Lombardo!*"

The triangle between my father, the clarinet and myself, though portending the evolution of our relationship, had no time to develop since I departed very soon thereafter for my *au pair* year in France, reluctantly leaving my Corvair in the care of Robert's ex-girlfriend Diana who, having for many years been a sort of 'big sister' to me, I implicitly trusted; but before I handed those precious keys over to her I drove one last time over to my dad's house to say good-bye. I was in the glow of my travel plans and he, sitting in front of the shelf containing, uniform and stamped in gold, the untouched leather bindings of his partially complete Franklin Library, betrayed by his conversation, the thoughts of which seemed to wander across his forehead as ponderously as a desert caravan looking wearily at the horizon, no awareness that I was about to leave the country for an entire year. When I got up to go he followed me onto the porch of his house and, staring blindly through his thick glasses, stood like a statue watching me as I pulled away. He remained in my rear-view mirror all the length of the long block, a tiny speck in a white shirt pathetically waving, as if a flag of surrender at dusk on a deserted battlefield.

Two weeks after I arrived in France my mother called to tell me, in her 'brace yourself' tone of voice, that he was in the hospital, recovering from an overdose of anti-depressants. I reacted to this news as if I were a child who can beautifully mimic the gestures of solemnity without understanding what they mean. *I was sad,* but my sadness had no realistic basis, it was an empty shell of an emotion applied to a man who, I suddenly realized, was little more to me than a symbol which, though I sporadically endowed it with importance, remained mysterious, my mother's anger obscuring it in a fog as thick as the magically conjured mist Merlin wrapped around Uther Pendragon so that he might enter the castle unnoticed and spend one night of passion with Igrain. After all, we had not occupied the same household since I was five years old. And though he had always lived, albeit with his new wife and children, very close by, and Fred, Robert, and I had seen him at least once a month, the estrangement constituent to divorce tended to strain our interviews and we, as if inhabitants on the outermost reaches of a kingdom long accustomed to self-governing, were offended when he attempted to assume his authority and give us some well-intentioned, but inevitably, and often *painfully,* uninformed advice. Regarding his current condition I told my French hosts that my father had suffered a heart attack and then, retiring early, I sat in my bedroom and wrote him letters filled with maladroit entreaties, in which every extravagant curve I added to my "I love you's" betrayed, when on the thin paper they dried into permanence, the well-meaning condescension of a mandatory affection born of a blood tie as formal in its rehearsal of tenderness as is the professional expression of concern a psychiatrist has for his patient. News of his progress reached me via my brother Robert, who returned from Mexico City and took it upon himself to 'manage' the situation for our side of the family and make a heroic effort to convince my father that life was, despite everything, worth living, a task, Robert recently confessed to me, more disheartening than anything he had ever faced. Apparently, though I was protected from this information at the time, after my father regained consciousness the first words he spoke, after motioning for Robert to draw near to his bed, were: "would you please bring me a gun".

Throughout this crisis my mother and I had several phone conferences during which she urged me to stay in France and finish out my year as planned; *things were returning to normal,* she assured me, and in fact my father *was* soon released from intensive care to the psychiatric unit, and from there not long after to his home where he quickly improved and began to resume, at least in appearances, the duties of his former life. Knowing that *he did not want to live* was more ingredient of my father's spirit than I had ever before had access to and yet, battening my thoughts down to future hope, I could not bring myself to mention it. I kept on with my letters until late fall when in his silence my insensitivity settled and I, but for the occasional note, stopped writing him altogether.

Gradually I became acclimatized to my life in France and, though every once and a while I took out the mini slide of 'little red' that I stored for safe-keeping in my wallet and held it up to the light, the Paris Métro had, with its soothing rhythms and old smell, which I thought of as 'turn of the century ether', seduced me into nearly forgetting the charms of my beloved car. Then, just before Christmas, I received a letter from my mother that made me ashamed of my callous attitude. It was written, as she sometimes had a tendency to do, in the style of a suspenseful short story, but I, being not so skilled as she in the matter of narrative unfolding, will not attempt to reproduce it here except in the barest of summaries: one night, after she and Clyde had been asleep for some hours, the doorbell began ringing in that insistent and intrusive manner that has for its goal the awakening of any persons inside the house. My mother turned on the light to see that it was three a.m. at which point she, fearing some ill omen regarding Fred, who had become increasingly entangled in lawless ventures, hastily donned her velour robe and ran down the long hallway leading off of her bedroom to the front of the house. She opened the thick, wooden front door which, ever since the laying of the new plush carpet, dragged along the floor, nearly a quarter of an inch too long to easily clear the nape, and saw behind it two police officers who asked if they might speak with me. Impossible she said, my daughter is in France, and then, as she stood there stunned, they informed her, in proper order and according to regulation, that a vehicle registered to my name had been found out in front of Diana's apartment building, half-way on the sidewalk, glass smashed and frame bent, apparently the victim of a hit-and-run accident. And so it was that my first automotive love, my darling little Corvair, my font of *sensuous longing* and *nostalgic passions,* was retired from its motoring life for ever by, I presume, though no witnesses came forward, a drunk and reckless driver. Could nothing be done to save 'little red'? My mother assured me that no heroic measures could be morally justified as he had naught for hope of a normal life after coming out of the shop. As for my first car's final resting place, whether city dump or used automotive parts dealer I remain ignorant; you see, I wanted to remember him as he was on our final drive: a warm breeze coming in the open window, 'All or Nothing at All' on the radio, and my dad, a fading memory, disappearing in the rear-view mirror.

A few months after this unexpected loss, on an early morning in late February, in the tiny apartment where I had been living and working as the caretaker of two French boys, the phone rang its clear French ring and I opened my eyes somehow aware it was my mother. It was. She was calling to tell me that before the western sun had risen my father, no longer able to support his despair, had driven out to the Mexico Shop storage unit and, while still sitting in his car, shot himself in the head. *I witness the corpse with its dabbled hair, I note where the pistol has fallen.* Made mechanical by disbelief I hung up the phone, went into the kitchen and prepared the *petit déjeuner* for the boys. After they left for school and I threw myself into household chores. I fumbled in a barely restrained emotional control until late afternoon when, fragile with the expectation of my French woman's return, I accidentally dropped the iron and it split into two pieces. I knew that *Madame* would take the accident as a personal failure, two steps back in her project to rid me of the extravagant clumsiness that had been bred into me by my privileged and vulgar country.

Upon her return I timidly announced the accident. As the exasperation drew a pool of water into her eyes I burst into tears and told her about my father. The words were thick in my mouth, they seemed to dissolve reality and fix me permanently within their logic and within that moment, as if their articulation would sink me forever in the crease of that hideous leather couch, tears streaming off my chin, contorted into eternal grief like those unfortunate victims of burning ash in the ancient city of Pompeii. Patiently correcting my grammatical error in omitting the reflexive 'se' before the verb 'suicider', my French woman consoled herself with a display of decorative pity and then, very sweetly petting my hair as I sat there red and monstrous, she left off her scolding for a sort of imperial maternalism and insisted that I take a cure, whatever might suit my fancy, which was, at that moment, to be released from the confines of that eighth-floor apartment and attain the nearby wood.

The next thing I knew I was there, a tiny walking figure beneath the very tall trees who, understanding my instability, offered me up a very fine specimen of a branch which I made for awhile my walking stick and then, as if commanded by some higher force, used to write a message to my father in the moist, dark, earth. As I wrote I became aware that my father was very close by, extant in the ambient air, and then he was gone, drifting unanchored as an errant leaf, *all goes onward and outward, nothing collapses,* swept off forever into the white, February, sky.

Making Walks, Making Works

STUART MUGRIDGE *in conversation with* CHRISTINE KENNEDY

CK *Does your art practice exist in any sense in the external landscapes which you walk within? Is the walking itself part of the art, or does it or your other activities out there have material consequences which are art? Or then again perhaps there is the potential for the art that is the books returning to the landscape in some form, perhaps in performance or installation for instance?*

SM When I first started making work in this sort of way I did three pieces (one in Devon, one in Wales and one in Kent) where I made some form of written record of the walk and then went back and placed sections of the text at various points on the route. These texts were placed in boxes in two cases, and in the other case (Wales) wrapped in cloth and put into small kist-like chambers in the ground. I don't think any of them lasted long, due to cows, the elements, and vandals. More recently I have used (in 'Sites of Cultural and Natural Interest') small plastic waymarkers (like you get on long-distance paths) nailed to stiles and fences. These were to advertise the project (which was a residency with a local conservation group) and as part of the work in their own right.

On the whole though my work exists only in the form of the 'artists book'. The walking is done for a different reason to, say, Richard Long. His work is often about the walk as art work. I use walking to explore an area or to link places. More recently my works have been about moments on a walk ('MLW', 'Papillon', etc.), or employing the instruments of walking—maps and their symbols, etc—this last is mainly evident in a series of paintings I am working on.

Today, I'm not so keen on the idea of putting my work into the landscape. (In the case of the waymarkers I didn't mind as it was akin to what is already all over the landscape, on stiles, and gates, and this was part of the reason why I did it). I do like the idea, though, that a lot of my books can be taken back to the place where they were inspired from and used as a conceptual guide book.

Robert Smithson wrote in the early '70s: "Many parks and gardens are re-creations of the lost paradise or Eden, and not the dialectical sites of the present.

Parks and gardens are pictorial in their origin—landscapes created with natural materials rather than paint. The scenic ideals which surround our national parks are carriers for a nostalgia for heavenly bliss and eternal calmness. Apart from the ideal gardens of the past, and their modern counterparts—national and urban parks, there are the more infernal regions—slag heaps, strip mines and polluted rivers." Which of these categories of landscapes do your walks and books explore or derive from? Why do you gravitate to one kind of landscape or another?

I have tried to make work from an urban environment but it wasn't a success. The places I make work from tend to be the picturesque. Having said that I am completely aware that all parts of this island have been touched by human hands at some point, and many of my works have an element of man's impact on the landscape, and the way in which humans have tried to organise it. This could be anything from markers for shipping on a Cornish cliff ('Vrogue Rock') to cartography (which is just man trying to codify the landscape). I made 'Vrogue Rock' in 2000. The following text is taken from my website: "Vrogue Rock lies just off of Bass Point on The Lizard, Cornwall, England. Along a stretch of the eastern coast of The Lizard there are two sets of daymarks which, when aligned from the sea, give the position of Vrogue Rock—thus enabling sailors to avoid this treacherous rock. The book is comb-bound with a 'map' held in the back cover." The walk connects these daymarks.

In the 1980s, Craig Owens discussed the allegorical aspect of landscape, exploring how he saw allegory as a component of the contemporary fine art practices of land art at that time. Is allegory something which interests you, do you ever think of the landscape or the walk as being used in your books as a representation of 'something else', telling perhaps a moral story? A work of yours involves a hunter's spent gun cartridge which you had found and I felt that this might point a reader towards the idea that the landscape was a setting for some kind of morality play?

It is not often that my work has a moral behind it (although underlying most of the work there is a subtle 'look what we are doing to the world' message, but this could be for good or bad). The book you mention is 'Undwelt-in-Wood' which I made in 1995. On a simple level it was the record of a walk in the Weald but on another level it concerned hunting.

The walk was made in one of the 'remnants' of Anderida (Roman name for the ancient wood which once covered much of the Weald). This wood was once much feared and there were only a few routes passing through it—it was the haunt of dangerous wild animals, and man was uncertain of entering it. Today walking through the woods, much of the area is 'man-made' forest or farmed for rearing pheasants. It is now the animals that are scared to show themselves as illustrated in the text "dropping down to the woods/a deer vanishes into the thicket", and the inclusion of the shotgun cartridge.

Some of your earlier works use text more than your more recent ones. Please describe one or more of these, and include some extracts of the language used, and describe the composition process of this—where you found the language, or how you made it, or adapted it etc.

Yes, as I think I said there has been a shrinking of text content in my work as the years have gone by. I started by listing 'everything' I saw, smelt, heard, etc. Then there was the second period where I employed a sort of faux Haiku style—I still like this way of working, but my head doesn't seem to be thinking in the same way at the moment! The transition to the second period probably came with 'Steeplechase' (1993), about a short circular walk near my home in Kent. There are three pages of text which alternate in the direction one reads them—from the title page you go up the page to a cut-out through to the first page, where one reads downwards to a cut-out through to page two, etc. Here is a short extract (from page two):

Houses and barns—a dog barking
distant gun shots
'Road Closed'
A concrete track through fruit fields
a Magpie and a Jay in the thinned wood
The faint noise of a stream
'Electric Fence'
The sweet smell of silage

There is a combination of senses—smells, noises, sights—and two lines of 'found' text. This still has the air of a sensory collage gathered as I walked.

'Skyland (1994) I did in two formats. One format was a straight hardback book with photographs, each page being separated by a blank page to add air and space to the work. The other format was a fold-out printed on to acetate. The text on acetate is suspended between two card covers, and there is an horizon of grey ribbon when the piece is held taut (this is quite difficult as I constructed it to my proportions and I have quite a large span). This book has a much more pared-down text, here are some extracts (each extract being the content of a page):

> November morning, chilly east wind
> Grey. A hazy half-light

> pylons, tracks, lanes
> lines
> broad, deep furrows

> Grey

> wind rustling the ochre reeds
> 'Freight line' and 'Church (rems of)'
> swans fly in the dusk

Again there are the found texts, this time from the map, movement, weather references (this is a common observation in my works). There is also the page of geometric line observations, and an ambiguous 'grey'—referring mainly to the weather/light.

In April 1995 I made 'On The Ironside Line'. Again a hardback with pages of text, and at the back a fold-out of bird silhouettes. The work is mainly concerning this line of WW2 defences on the River Medway that were never used in anger, and now the only threat to them is from 'nature'. It is looking at the Medway Valley landscape through the eyes of a WW2 defence planner, so we have:

River Medway anti-tank ditch
Thin hedges and open fields
of the valley

Setting off it is 'Humid / An oppressive sky' but when we reach a pillbox it is 'Cool inside' and the text ends 'Quiet and still' in stark contrast to their intended life.

In 1997 I made a very small work called 'Between Stream and Field' about a moment encountered walking across the fields to work. The text if I remember correctly goes:

Stopping to examine
fescue or false oat grass

in the closeness of the morning
a dragonfly rises

It is from around this time that most of my work has contained minimal text. For instance 2000's 'Swirl How Cairn' about a walk to the top of a peak in the Coniston Fells, Cumbria. The text is 'looking at the map to see the view' printed faintly on white tissue paper. [The spelling, punctuation, and justification of all the extracts is as in the original except for 'Between Stream and Field']

Is the choice of typeface for your textual elements very important? For many who make small editions and artist books this is a very important area of taste and judgment. What kind of decision making process goes on with this for you?

Originally I chose the typeface to be sympathetic with the mood of the work, but since about 1997/8 I have mainly stuck to using some form of Gill Sans (plain, bold, italic, etc.). It is a fairly neutral font, and I like its similarity to that of the text on OS maps. Thinking of the earlier works in 'On the Ironside Line' I used a type that mimicked a typewriter, to give a feel of wartime intelligence messages. 'Steeplechase' used quite an old-fashioned style of text to give it a warm feel.

Tell me about your most recent completed work or works. I would be interested to learn about your working methods in these—inspiration, techniques, materials and so on. I would also like to know what prompted these. Is it, for instance, that you just felt it was time to make a new work, or that you were invited to do such and such, or what?

My two most recent books, 'NTL/VTC' and 'Papillon', are both references to moments or encounters on a walk that I made. Sometimes I make a walk with the strict intention of making work, other times the idea appears during or after a walk. They are both simple ideas, using colours and textures to represent things. There is virtually no text (aside from the title and edition details) in either of them.

'Papillon' refers to the sighting of a small blue butterfly whilst standing at the top of a mountain in the Pyrenees with a very strong wind blowing, and it deals with how such delicate creatures survive in such a harsh environment. The book consists of tissue paper pages between sandpaper pages, with a hessian cover.

'NTL/VTC' comes from time spent around the Helford River in Cornwall. It is a book of roughly torn muddy coloured pastel paper pages and one clean white page. In addition to the title it contains the text 'egretta garzetta' and a tick box. The book is about these brilliantly coloured (and clean) birds which live amongst the estuary mud, and contains the reference to birdspotting books. The cover is made of a rubberised waterproof material. I knew what sort and colour of material I wanted—old-fashioned groundsheet stuff—and so went to a local army surplus shop. They didn't have any groundsheets but had some army-issue ponchos, from the German and English forces. To the amusement of the chap in the shop I chose the German one because the colour was better. So the cover is made of German army-issue poncho.

Southborough—Sheffield, November 2002—March 2003

Books in Print

Sea I—Wave (2003) Edn of 6. £36 ea.

Crag Head (2003) Edn of 12. £8 ea.

Papillon (2002) Edn of 12. £15 ea.

NTL/VTC (2002) Edn of 12. £22 ea.

Seven Short Walks (2002) Edn of 200. £10 ea.

Seven Short Walks Magnifier (2002) Edn of 30. £3 ea.

Où est 602? (2001) Edn of 12. £22 ea.

Cupiditas Videndi (2001) Edn of 4. £28 ea.

Sites of Cultural & Natural Interest (2001) Edn of 1200. £2 ea.

SNCI—Waymarker (2001) Edn of 500. 50p ea.

Walk in a Valley of Vision (2000) Edn of 8. £34 ea.

Vrogue Rock (2000) Edn of 6. £12 ea.

Carrick Lûz (1999) Edn of 18. £2 ea.

On the Ironside Line (1995) Edn of 18. £15 ea.

Steeplechase (1993) Edn of 30. £4 ea.

Walking the Yellow Brick Road:
A Pedestrian Account of J.H. Prynne's *Poems*

JEREMY NOEL-TOD

> The street that is the
> sequence of man
> is the light of his
> most familiar need,
> to love without being stopped for some im-
> mediate bargain, to be warm and tired
> without some impossible flame in the heart.
> As I walked up the hill this evening and felt
> the rise bend up gently against me I knew
> that the void was gripped with concentration.
> Not mine indeed but the sequence of fact,
> the lives spread out
> 'The Common Gain, Reverted'

Preamble

> Verse is a pedestrian taking you over the ground.[1]
> T.E. Hulme

There is a suspicion among commentators that J.H. Prynne does not write for the man in the street. His amber-wrapped, not-quite-collected *Poems* (or 'yellow brick' as the author is said to have called it) begins, in 1968, with a demanding new poetic which has only increased in obliquity and compression. Surveying critics have tended to conclude that, finally, it is not a brick in a road but a wall—the churlish, from page one; others, more sympathetic, from any point after the first third or so. In the accounts of the latter, Prynne turns away from the neo-Wordsworthianism of his early work in favour of a supreme (albeit ongoing) impeding of the reader, by which the author stands revealed as a Whiz of a Wiz if ever a Wiz there was, and the reader learns that we are not in Kansas now, Toto. For some, this is to be regretted; for others, it is his greatest achievement. At such an impasse, there is a danger of debate breaking down into a quarrel over who lacks a heart / brains / courage. I want instead to counterpoise a claim for an essential consistency in

89

Prynne's project, which I will treat as unapologetically Wordsworthian in its ambition to educate through poetry. In Prynne's own words, 'Wordsworth, when he wrote what looks to us like lyrics, was simply teaching what he knew in the most directly didactic effective method he knew how'.[2] I will do this by following a figure which recurs both in Prynne's poetry and critical prose: walking as primary knowledge of a reality that—like the rise of a hill—resists our too-easy progress, and so connects us to our human commonality.[3]

Prynne's early formulation of a poetics, 'Resistance and Difficulty' (1962), proposes that 'the concept of resistance may provide an alternative criterion to intelligibility'.[4] Through the experience of resistance the world is 'found to exist… in all its complex variousness'.[5] Concomitantly, the work of art which resists coherently (and is not merely perversely 'difficult') *shows* the world to exist as complexly and variously as the artist has found it. This, of course, is not so different to other modernist credos—Wallace Stevens's 'Man Carrying Thing', for example: 'The poem must resist the intelligence / Almost successfully'. But the premise of Prynne's resistance is more materialist than Stevens's ideal of a 'supreme fiction'. These poems resist by taking words not as biddable symbols but contoured terrain, correspondent to the life-world figured in English as 'the street'—'the sequence of fact, / the lives spread out'. Their composition does not streamline cognition of this world but encounters it. At the expense of considering the many original effects produced by such a poetic, but in the hope of providing some fingerposts, this essay will concentrate on those passages which run between the inductive cul-de-sacs of Prynne's resistance with clear insistence about 'the sequence of fact' presented, and its relationship to 'the lives spread out'.

To claim intelligibility for this poetry is not to say that it can be cakewalked as the kind of contemporary lyric that presents the personalised perceptions of one man out on a poetic stroll—usually, as Prynne has put it, in 'a landscape or environment not containing other beings that we can conceive of as living—over days and weeks—their own, various lives'.[6] The basic human experience of walking down the street is an experience in which the immediately intelligible (one's own route) shades off into the unknown (the earth, the sky, other people's routes). As such, it is the ground bass for the complexities of *Poems*:

'In my own figure and shared by the stately non-involvement of people in the street there is a difficult motion which in my wildest dreams I would not allow to be improved'.[7] Prynne's 1962 essay proposes the imagination as 'one of our most valuable modes of access to the resistance beyond our several difficulties', in implicit opposition to a self-alienated rationalism.[8] When Descartes, in his Second Meditation ('Of the Nature of the Human Mind; and that it is Easier to Know than the Body'), looks out of the window, and sees 'men passing in the street', he doubts even this knowledge: 'and yet, what do I see from this window, other than hats and cloaks, which can cover ghosts or dummies who move only by means of springs?' It is only rational judgement, Descartes concludes—and not 'imagination, or the senses'—which tells him that these men are not machines.[9] By contrast, in the first poem of *Poems*, 'The Numbers', 'walking is a white charge / in the bones we look at'. To see men walking is to experience, in a flash, the pre-cognitive apprehension of their equal reality. Thereafter, walking recurs as a figure which insists upon, and refreshes, this intuition of co-being, even as the poetry traverses the slippery slope from walking as rectitude to walking—all over—in domination.

'Or feel it / as you walk'

The perspective of the walker is adopted by a number of poems in Prynne's first collection, *Force of Circumstance and Other Poems* (1962). The book is not included in *Poems*, but its short, tightly-worked lyrics give a first statement of themes developed by the free stride of the later work. 'Street Plan' begins:

> Some minds are perpetually flooded
> By these grooved intersections, plotting
> The city's anonymous stance.

This passive 'stance' is contrasted with intimations of vitality crowding upon the walker:

> A possible
> Scene, curbed into latency,
> Shouts urgently through the soles of the feet.

The opposition is of the concrete actual and the concrete-covered possible, with the pun on 'kerb' drawn out in the next imperative sentence: 'Walk then / Carefully, over the narrowing pavements.' The speaker concludes by declaring his apprehension of some 'remoter purpose' in 'many / Large cities':

> Swaying with huge, sightless tides,
> All my pockets awash with broken glass.

From the 'some' whose minds are 'flooded' by the present fact of the city, the poem has moved to the point of view of a citizen himself feeling flooded and swayed by an image implying violent change to the window-lined scene of the street.

There is certainly fear, of damage, in Prynne's pocketful of glass, but also an excitement at the urgent human 'tide' of the city, which is not at all the flâneurial modernist despair of T.S. Eliot's *The Waste Land*: 'A crowd flowed over London Bridge, so many, / I had not thought death had undone so many.' Prynne's city is not a waste place but a latent one. 'The Holy City' in *The White Stones* (1969) experiences the same act of walking—and pausing—in an urban environment as a kind of earthly Paradise:

> Come up to it, as you stand there
> that the wind is quite warm on the sides
> of the face.

'Where we go' at such a moment is, importantly, nowhere: 'a loved side of the temple, / a place for repose, a concrete path'. Prynne has been a Fellow of Gonville and Caius College since the 1960s, so his 'side of the temple' may well be a Cambridge chapel, enclosing a concrete-pathed grass quadrangle. In the poem, however, it is transformed from any particular spot into an apprehension—'come up to'—of the body. Stopping, the walker feels himself to be a three-dimensional man, not merely a forward vector, with a 'face' which also has sides (and temples):

There's no mystic moment involved: just
    that we are
    is how, each
    severally, we're
    carried into
the wind which makes no decision and is
a tide, not taken. I saw it
    and love is
    when, how &
    because we
    do: you
could call it Ierusalem or feel it
as you walk, even quite jauntily, over the grass.

What the poet sees is not a landscape but an emotion, 'love' in the widest sense, of being one of mankind, which is 'The Holy City'. The poem declines to appropriate this apprehension to a historical name ('Ierusalem') which might enlist it into a sectarian cause. Instead, the verse's tidal fluctuations rise to the rhythm of the last and longest line, which picks up the dactylic foot in 'Ierusalem' and walks off with it, '*even quite jauntily, over* the *grass*'. At the same time, the quaint, colloquial adverb 'jauntily' leads us back etymologically (through 'gently' and 'Gentile') to 'gens': the widest possible tribe. The divisions of which *Force of Circumstance* analytically treads the boundaries—between 'one' and 'some', mind and body, city and country—are here blended into a poetic speech both more resistant and more plain: 'we are', 'each / severally'. The elevation of that—walking on air, even, '*over* the grass' as Prynne puts it in an essay from the same period, it is 'joy as the complete ground gathered underfoot'[10]—is available to each, severally, not just the zealot.

'The end is a carpet on / which we walk'

Reviewing Charles Olson's *Maximus Poems IV, V, VI* in 1968, Prynne noted that in the development of the sequence with the history of Gloucester, Massachusetts, 'the critical necessity is to keep the moral structure of immediate knowledge from damage during its transition to the schedule of city-settlement'.[12] The poetic argument of 'The Holy City' is for the same necessity: to recognize the moral primacy of 'a concrete path' of purposiveness—love—on a concrete path. As Prynne remarked in a 1971 lecture on *Maximus IV, V, VI*, 'Oh yes, I am an absolute predestinarian in that sense. I believe utterly in that it is man's destiny to bring love to the universe, I mean, to fulfill the universe's potential for love.'[11] The validity of this elated, immediate knowledge of the human is underwritten, however, by its opposite movement: down to earth, which is the other knowledge, of non-human reality—the 'rise' of the street that 'bends up gently against' each member of the walking gens, resisting with a force of its own.

> As you drag your feet or simply being
> slow, the ground is suddenly interesting;
> not as metaphysic as the grave maybe,
> that area which claims its place like
> a shoe.

'A Gold Ring Called Reluctance', from *Kitchen Poems* (1968), is the darker, more discursive shadow poem to 'The Holy City'. It begins in the same way—walking and pausing ('simply being / slow')—but with its eyes cast down, at the 'dust', and then 'the dead', who are 'a necessity to us, / keeping our interest from being too much / about birth.' Awareness of the dead beneath our feet attaches ballast to the fantasy that we are on the way to some more satisfactory city, some 'end' or Messianic 'birth' over the horizon. Again, this expands upon a lyric from *Force of Circumstance*, 'To Petrarch, on Mount Ventoux', in which a 'lowered gaze' wards off the enchantment of the 'prospect... of what's to come'. Rather, 'A Gold Ring' contends, 'The end is a carpet on / which we walk': the condition of mortality is the world already spread comfortably beneath us. If we could feel this as we walk, the poem suggests in conclusion, we might recover 'this / fact we call place'—which 'grows daily more remote'— as 'The ground on which we pass, / moving our feet, less excited by travel.' *On* which, not *over* which (in the magic-carpet age of air travel); 'pass[ing]' and 'moving our feet' as living, not passing through.

'We walk / in beauty down the street'

The paradoxes which impinge upon the motion of these early poems, already making them 'difficult' to an unusual degree, are manifold. They revive a Romantic tradition of poetry—the conversation poems of the hill-walking young Wordsworth and Coleridge—radically turned against that tradition's pastoralised debasement; and they practice a poetic of historical scholarship while according moral primacy to phenomenologically 'immediate' knowledge. In the words of 'Die a Millionaire', 'The first essential is to take knowledge / back to the springs'. They are, in short, idealistically anti-idealist. The strain shows more clearly in Prynne's next major collection, *Brass* (1971). Here, the 'moral structure of immediate knowledge' as experienced by the contemplative walking subject is displaced from the centre of the poetry by the clamour of other kinds of knowledge in the public sphere:

> 1. Steroid metaphrast
> 2. Hyper-bonding of the insect
> 3. 6% memory, etc
> any other rubbish is mere political rhapsody, the
> gallant lyricism of the select, breasts & elbows,
> > what
> else is allowed by the verbal smash-up piled
> under foot. Crush   tread   trample   distinguish

At this junction, 'L'Extase de M. Poher' appears to reject the 'gallant lyricism' of jaunty feeling—knowledge taken back to the spring in the step—for a poetry *of* rubbish. This may be read as the more violent rhetorical return of the allegiance to the 'dust' (and 'scrap') underfoot in 'A Gold Ring'. The violence, however, now becomes its own explanation, a 'verbal smash-up' from which the poet does not walk free or 'distinguish' himself. The gapped words of the last line explicitly don't distinguish between treading everything together and sorting it all out. Rather, their sequencing suggests that the project of distinguishing occurs only once everything has already been trampled to pieces; as if the very project to dissect the world into bullet-pointed branches of knowledge were itself, by Wordsworthian paradox, implicated in a murderous act of destruction.

> What more can be done. We walk
> > in beauty down the street, we tread
> the dust of our wasted fields.
> > > > 'The Ideal Star-Fighter', *Brass*

Although exhortation in Prynne's poetry to walk 'carefully' begins to be replaced by exhibition of the damage 'under foot' in *Brass*, this doesn't mean that the poetry abandons its allegiance to the moral structure of immediate knowledge. Rather, the writing increasingly presents patches of hazard where readers must distinguish their own way, testing constructions for reliability and emphasis. On one level, 'We walk / in beauty down the street' may be a sincere statement, consistent with some of Prynne's more passionate prose remarks. But its winking allusion to Byron ('She walks in beauty, like the night') is a complication to give us pause. What does it mean to 'walk *in* beauty', collectively? To 'walk in' an abstract or metaphorical state—grace, righteousness, or darkness—is the Biblical language of the poet's Puritan ancestor, William Prynne, when, for example, he quotes Proverbs 2.13 against those who, by going to the theatre, 'leave the pathes of uprightnesse, to walke in the wayes of darknesse'.[13] To say 'we walk in beauty' seems a more antinomian vision, yet it is laced with irony: do we 'walk in beauty' narcissistically, in love with ourselves as Byron is with his mistress? Or do we even 'walk in beauty' like unseen dogshit, treading through it like 'the dust of our wasted fields'? And what, here, is the agreed definition of 'beauty'?

Donald Davie has glossed the argument of 'The Ideal Star-Fighter' as a rejection of 'the moral blackmail which the ecologist's propaganda exerts and depends upon'.[14] This is not to say that it rejects the evidence of ecological damage, but rather the whimsical moralism of doing 'your bit' for 'the planet'. The lack of scale in such a phrase perpetuates the remoteness from responsibility to which Prynne opposes the figure of responsive walking. Consequently, the apocalyptic pathos of 'we tread the dust of our wasted fields' is also to be distrusted. Are they really 'wasted' into sterile 'dust', or merely good dry soil wasted by incompetent use of the ground on which we live? Etymologically, 'tread' is only a step from 'trade', which continues unabated down the street. We only walk in such sighing, self-pitying beauty ('What more can be done') because, as another poem in *Brass* puts it, we have made 'cash... a principle of nature' ('A New Tax on the Counter-Earth'), thereby commodifying the landscape itself. Going for a walk in the spirit of Wordsworth now is a leisurely penance which does not avoid complicity. 'A New Tax...' notes the inscription from a memorial plaque typically affixed to a bench along such a walk:

"The spot was the one which
he loved best in all the world."

'And such affection curdles the effort to be just', Prynne comments. The impulse towards a 'just' knowledge of the world has become, by the absurdly acquisitive idea of loving one 'spot' best of all, 'the rightness of wayward sentiment'. This, says the poem, is what lights 'the horizon'—like a phantasmal holy city—and towards which, by implication, we walk in darkness.

'Renewing and walking'

The theme of vestigial harm done to the whole—'the land is cleared // by the footprint of a quiet man / with a snack in his wife's / pocket' (*Down Where Changed*, 1979)—spreads through the poetry that follows, as it sardonically falls into step with the high street 'footfall' of accelerated consumerism: 'You stamp about / looking for more cheap cuts and square deals' (*News of Warring Clans*, 1977). As Prynne's resistance to the reader increases in irony, it is tempting to resist in return by ascribing to the author of such texts the rejection of all heartfelt impulses. To do so, though, would be to miss the poetry's openness to emotion. One of the best pieces of criticism on Prynne's later work begins with a 'hazy affective response', and proceeds on the reasonable assumption that there are material and emotional footholds to be found in the verbal scrambling.[15] Jay Basu concludes that the idea of 'reading' in the sequence *Red D Gypsum* (1998) 'becomes not a matter of cognitive process … a retreat into the private internal sanctity of our minds' but a 'physical action', like 'walking', which investigates 'the paradigmatic moment of impulsive feeling'.[16] Plain corroboration that Prynne remains susceptible to such feelings is available on page 380 of *Poems*, which gives the text of *Jie ban mi Shi Hu* (1992). Authorship of this poem in Chinese has been cited in the English-speaking world as proof of Prynne's inhuman perversity. In fact, a readily-available translation reveals something like the surprising opposite:

Stepping upon the bridge to push open ancient ages
Standing on the bridge and watch the ancient views
Green mosses cover deserted gardens

With a friend, to talk in heartfelt words
In a rainy day, to cup fragrant leaves
Long echoing sweetly in the heart

The translator, Li Zhimin, notes that in an ingenious (and 'Western individualis[t]') twist, Prynne's handwritten Chinese characters may be read in four directions.[17] The emotional matrix, however, remains the same: 'heartfelt' walking and talking. The same matrix occurs in *Pearls That Were* (1999). This sequence is prefaced by what seems to be a diaristic nature note, in the manner of Dorothy Wordsworth. Having described how gossamer threads spread over 'ferny leaf-blades' shimmered in the evening sun, it concludes: 'we both remarked on it...' As in the Chinese poem, a close walking companion is implied. This image of companionable walking returns at the end of the sequence (in a final lyric which also begins 'Stepping'):

To talk to and fro with each
    other renewing and walking,
step for a span wayward in
    heart to heart breaking.

Much like waves upon a shore
    whose day approaches,
her time running to meet
    with joy the face it touches.

And word upon word, step
    by next step regaining
they'll walk and talk, wisely
    flicker some hope remaining.

Long shadows flicker over familiar phrases here, as a 'heart to heart' turns painfully intimate. Shakespeare's image of mortality is invoked ('Like as the waves make towards the pebbled shore, / So do our minutes hasten to their end', *Sonnets* 60); and the 'hope remaining' in the last line seems to be 'flickersome' at best; at worst, only 'some'—as in 'some hope', meaning none.

'Won't you walk there'

Importantly, the phrases of hope and despair at the end of *Pearls that Were* can't be plucked singly from their string. Prynne's *Poems* invites a similarly continuous reading; not as 'the / maze of a shining path... without a break' (*Unanswering Rational Shore*, 2001) but dialectically, back and forth. This, finally, is what the figure of walking stands for in Prynne: to feel, by participation, the polarities of the resistant whole, in motion—to be moved by hope and despair. The title of the sequence *Biting the Air* (2003) openly indicates one of its concerns: the powerlessness of contemporary popular resistance, imaged as a 'muted / counter-march' in the first stanza. Crowds walking through London against the war in Iraq chanting 'not in our name' stopped nothing, a point made explicitly by the uncollected poem 'Refuse Collection' (dated 08.05.2004—the week of the Abu Ghraib prison torture pictures—and published in *Quid* 13): 'In our name long-term marching as, to / a holy city'. Here, Prynne again refuses to distinguish the refuse collected underfoot, instead indicting the whole 'holy city' in which we live 'as' that which also marches now through the Middle East, as crusading Christian soldiers once to Ierusalem.

The politics of this are bleak; the rapid-response poetic, flatly sarcastic. A fuller, more resistant figuring of the same situation comes at the end of *Biting the Air*. Here, walking returns as the first necessary step into acknowledgement of the 'im-/mediate' common world. The same necessity informs Prynne's 2002 comments on Paul Celan. Having declared 'It is high time to be crude' about Celan's sense of his historical 'destiny' as a post-Holocaust Jewish poet, Prynne elaborates:

> Somewhere in between the exacting sparsity of lexical reduction and the unsayable enormity of vast crimes lies the everyday political world, of what it is possible to do: the crimes to be found here are no less fearful and oppressive for being idiomatic to the day-to-day. Who can doubt that the prisoner of Ramallah is locked into heroic ignominy by a pursuit of vengeance, one itself avenged by daily self-sacrifice, one killing after another; and that the unsolved hatred and misery of camps and settlements comprise the long but evident

shadow of what for Celan was the memorial project of
his writing life...[18]

The passage proposes that Celan, like Yasser Arafat (besieged, in 2002, in
his compound in Ramallah), is implicated by 'heroic' high-mindedness
in Holy City narratives which now clash around the actual streets of
Jerusalem: 'the ordinary world in which not quite innocent people
(we, they, and us) dwell unpoetically upon the earth, and terminate in
anguish there'.[19] The force of this insistence on connection across 'the
ordinary world' is the force of the figure of walking as it recurs at the
end of *Biting the Air*. 'Get clear of some ever bad / muck on your shoes'
the final section commands ironically, an image of the upwardly mobile
West attempting to walk away from what its high streets 'ever' walk in:
the 'muck', cognate with the 'meek' who have not inherited the earth,
but who now make its trainers. Yet the poem seems also to allow that
in continuing (as Hölderlin said) to live poetically upon the earth—and
how can we not, when the root of 'poetry' is 'to make'—we are 'Still
ever born to make' things differently, renewing and walking:

> Don't you yet notice
> a shimmer on bad zero, won't you walk there
> and be the shadow unendurably now calibrated.

Prynne still knows how to walk offstage in the grand manner, and
here once more puts his foot down, in a sentence which indicts the
disingenuousness of not noticing the smoke and mirrors of economic
abstraction, rather than walking 'there' with the shadow—that is,
the spectral, mortal human other unavoidably linked to one's own
existence—whose life is 'unendurably now calibrated' somewhere along
the single, transglobal, rising and falling, 'street that is / the sequence
of man'.

*We are grateful to J.H. Prynne for permission to quote from his poems in this
essay. They are published in the volume* Poems *(expanded edition, 2005; Tarset,
Northumberland: Bloodaxe Books Ltd & Fremantle, W.A.: Fremantle Arts Centre
Press.)*

I am indebted to Nate Dorward's online bibliography: (www.ndorward.com/poetry/articles_etc/prynne-checklist.htm) for the forms of reference given below for articles by Prynne originally printed in unpaginated and / or undated numbers of *The English Intelligencer*.

Notes

[1] T.E. Hulme, 'Romanticism and Classicism', in *Speculations: Essays on Humanism and the Philosophy of Art*, ed. Herbert Read (London: Routledge and Kegan Paul, second edition 1936; repr. 1987), p.135.

[2] 'On *Maximus IV, V, VI*', *Iron* (October 1971), n.p. Available online at: www.charlesolson.ca/files/prynnelecture1.htm

[3] The moral import of this topos was first noticed by Donald Davie in 1973: 'in Prynne's poems man saves or at least preserves himself always and only by moving patiently on and over the surface of a landscape' (*Thomas Hardy and British Poetry*, p.128).

[4] 'Resistance and Difficulty', *Prospect* 5, 1962, 26–30 (p.27).

[5] ibid, p.30.

[6] 'from a letter', *Mica* 5, Winter 1962, 2–3, 28 (p.2).

[7] 'About Warning an Invited Audience (obliquely arising from George Dowden's *Letter to English Poets*)', *English Intelligencer*, 3rd ser. 2 [c. 22 Nov. 1967]: n.p.

[8] 'Resistance and Difficulty', p.30.

[9] René Descartes, *Discourse on Method and The Meditations*, trans. by F.E. Sutcliffe (London: Penguin, 1968), pp. 110–112.

[10] 'A Pedantic Note in Two Parts', *English Intelligencer* 2nd ser., c. June 1967: 346–51 (p. 351).

[11] Review of Charles Olson's *Maximus Poems IV, V, VI*, *The Park* 4/5 (Summer 1969), 64–66. Available online at : www.charlesolson.ca/files/prynnereview.htm

[12] 'On *Maximus IV, V, VI*', n.p.

[13] William Prynne, *Histrio-Mastix* (1632; repr. 1974, New York: Garland), p.384.

[14] Donald Davie, *Thomas Hardy and British Poetry*, (London: Routledge and Kegan Paul, 1973), p. 180.

[15] Jay Basu, 'The Red Shift: Trekking J.H. Prynne's *Red D Gypsum*', *Cambridge Quarterly*, Vol. 30, No.1, 2001, 19–36 (p. 19).

[16] Basu, p.26.

[17] Li Zhimin, 'Four Different Ways of Looking at J.H. Prynne's Chinese Poem—A Harmony of English and Chinese Cultures', *Quid* 7a (April 2001), 14–18 (pp. 15–16). Available online at: www.geocities.com/barque_press/quid7a.pdf
An alternative English translation is available in Birgitta Johansson, *The*

Engineering of Being: An Ontological Approach to J. H. Prynne (Uppsala: Umeå University, 1997), pp.190–1.

[18] 'Es Stand Auch Geschrieben: Jean Bollack and Paul Celan', *CCCP* 12 (2002), 104–6 (p.106). Available online (with some errors) at: www.cccp-online.org/archive/cccp12/page_49.html

[19] 'Es Stand Auch Geschrieben', p.106.

Gait Technology: Some Remarks on Walking and Writing

MALCOLM PHILLIPS

> Pour l'étranger de notre temps la reconnaissance est impossible.[1]
>
> Rimbaud, 'Villes'

> Battez-vous, faites des sports, des voyages, des guerres mais surtout ne retombez pas dans une philosophie que nous connaissons trop: le simulacre du mouvement de foules successivement unanimistes ... Quand vos constructions simulent le plus la vie, c'est l'idéal de l'ingénieur que vous suivez. Vous restez dans l'Objet qui se meut à la manière de tous les simulacres, qu'il vous faut alors douer d'une sensibilité.
> Vous marchez véritablement à la mort.[2]
>
> Robert Delaunay

'Since ancient times', writes Roger Gilbert, 'poetry and walking have seemed to go hand in hand'.[3] Gilbert wishes to establish 'the walk poem' as a genre where the 'form and function' of walk and poem are seen to be intimately related. In this analysis, 'the walk poem' offers access to ephemeral, physical and everyday aspects of reality-as-walk while maintaining the intensity and the shaping limits of a timeless, artifactual act of writing. Gilbert invokes Baudelaire's often quoted definition of modernity as 'the ephemeral, the fugitive, the contingent, the half of art whose other half is the eternal and the immutable' but strangely fails to mention what every other critic of walking and writing in recent times has taken from *Le peintre de la vie moderne*, namely the figure of the *flâneur*. As for Baudelaire's poetry, Gilbert deems it too taken up with the eternal and the timeless to be considered walk poetry, and traces instead a genealogy stretching back 'to Yahweh's walk "in the garden at the breezy time of day,"' on through the works of Theocritus, Virgil, Dante and Spenser, down to Wordsworth's 'An Evening Walk', where the genre achieves 'a kind of fulfilment' before tripping lightly across the Atlantic Ocean to become a solely American affair:

103

Not only does the rougher, less cultivated landscape of nineteenth-century America lend itself to the kind of close descriptive treatment developed in eighteenth century English poetry, but the very attitude towards experience that American writers hold leads them to take up with new vigor the mode of representation that in England effectively ends with Wordsworth.[4]

In the twentieth century, American poets are presented with a new landscape to cultivate, namely 'the middle ground between Whitman's barbaric yawp and Thoreau's journalism'.[5] The rest of Gilbert's book is taken up with an assessment of their pioneering endeavour. In a sharp and wide-ranging survey of critical treatments of walking and writing in English literature, Anne D. Wallace comments that

> ... although Gilbert thoroughly explicates what he regards as the inherent formal similarities between a walk and a poem—sequentiality, the possibility of continued outward movement and thought contained and intensified within a definite frame, and so forth— he assumes a Wordsworthian contiguous universe in which walking's physical continuities translate directly into temporal, spatial, and spiritual (or intellectual) continuities, and *so* generate text.[6]

What Wallace passes over is the extent to which this 'universalizing' account, as she terms it, is in fact one more instance in American criticism of the performance of a transatlantic shift in the global economy of culture, reminiscent of Harold Rosenberg's 'Parable of American Painting', where British 'Redcoats' are picked off by 'naked Indians and coon-skinned trappers' because 'they were such extreme European professionals' that they failed to recognise the American terrain of guerrilla warfare:

> The Redcoats fall, expecting at any moment to enter upon the true battlefield, the soft rolling greenswards prescribed by the canons of their craft and presupposed

by every principle that makes warfare intelligible to
the soldier of the eighteenth century.[7]

Rosenberg's argument is that 'Redcoatism' and 'Coonskinism' have
persisted as attitudes to the artistic inheritance of the New World, but
for my purposes its most interesting feature is that once more, albeit in
very different sense, the shift in power and wealth, which leaves Europe
behind in the eighteenth century once more, is seen to occur as figures
walk through a landscape.

It is ironic, therefore, that Michel de Certeau, writing some twenty
years after Rosenberg, should choose to begin his chapter on 'Marches
dans la Ville' in *L'invention du quotidien* on the 110th floor of the World
Trade Center. Certeau does not consider any intervening unit between
the urban and the global: the nation state does not so much as merit
a mention. The WTC 'n'est que la plus monumentale des figures de
l'urbanisme occidental'.[8] In fact, as the most manifest aspect of the
contemporary panopticon, it seeks to specialise the act of recognition
beyond a Redcoat's dream:

> La tour de 420 mètres qui sert de proue à Manhattan
> continue à construire la fiction qui crée des lecteurs,
> qui mue en lisibilité la complexité de la ville et fige en
> un texte transparent son opaque mobilité.[9]

De Certeau's interest is in power relations as they are played out
between stronger forces of interest and weaker constituencies such as
'l'homme ordinaire' to whom *L'invention du quotidien* is dedicated. He
makes a distinction between the *stratégies* deployed by the strong and
the *tactiques* improvised by the weak:

> J'appelle *stratégie* le calcul (ou la manipulation) des
> rapports de forces qui devient possible à partir du
> moment où un sujet de vouloir et de pouvoir (une
> entreprise, une armée, une cité, une institution
> scientifique) est isolable. Elle postule *un lieu* susceptible
> d'être circonscrit comme *un propre* et d'être la base d'où
> gérer les relations avec *une extériorité* de cibles ou de
> menaces (les clients ou les concurrents, les ennemis, la

campagne autour de la ville, les objectifs et objets de la recherche, etc.) [...] j'appelle *tactique* l'action calculée que détermine l'absence d'un propre [...] La tactique n'a pour lieu que celui de l'autre. Aussi doit-elle jouer avec le terrain qui lui est imposé tel que l'organise la loi d'une force étrangère.[10]

In this context, we can see the WTC as a *stratégie* which delimits a place: for de Certeau, walking about the city becomes a *tactique* by means of which that imposed terrain is made unreadable to the 'sujet de vouloir et de pouvoir' who deploys such strategies. De Certeau defines a 'rhétorique de la marche' which employs synecdoche and asyndeton: spatial elements come to stand for a totality ('le meuble en vente dans une vitrine vaut pour une rue entière ou un quartier'), and this process of selection in itself ruptures the continuities of a coherent, mappable city, offering instead 'l'ellipse de lieux conjonctifs'.[11]

Various attempts have been made to bring this analysis to bear on the 'walk poetry' of Frank O'Hara (although not by Gilbert), notably by Hazel Smith in *Hyperscapes in the Poetry of Frank O'Hara: Difference / Homosexuality / Topography* and Susan Rosenbaum in 'Frank O'Hara, *Flâneur* of New York'. Whether we find ourselves in sympathy with Certeau or not, there are problems with this. On the one hand, inasmuch as de Certeau's work is concerned with the empowering nature of what Jeremy Ahearne translates as the 're-employment' of elements of writing by the reader in ways that the author could not have foreseen, it seems only fitting that an analysis of walking which invokes the figure of a 'poetic geography' should be brought back to the discussion of poetry: but on the other hand, de Certeau's work, like that of the Situationists also invoked by Rosenbaum, is concerned with actual spatial practices in everyday life and involves a highly critical attitude towards literary culture.[12] There is surely an irony to the idea that an analysis which so emphasises discontinuity and unreadability should find itself adopted as part of a critical attempt to 'read' poems about walking, an attempt furthermore which is made in the name of a 'sujet de vouloir et de pouvoir', the university. This is a problem for de Certeau's own thinking as an intellectual, but it is doubly problematic for anyone attempting to translate his ideas into academic practice. Such translations take their place in a wider evolution of strategies to address the tactic of walking: since the destruction of the WTC, it has been announced that the Defense Advance Research Projects Agency in the U.S. has been involved in the development of "gait technology' which aims to move beyond face-recognition technology and purportedly identify people by the way they walk'.[13]

At this point I can finally get around to my epigraph from Delaunay's polemic against the Futurists. Timothy Mathews illustrates how 'Delaunay interprets the Futurist enterprise as a passive worship of the present, a naïve belief in the power of the imitation—albeit an undermined and subversive imitation—of speed and movement'.[14] In contrast, Delaunay's rival conception of simultaneity 'creates and initiatives [sic] movement itself by manipulating volume', according to Mathews. I propose that we see the asserted continuities between walking and writing in the work of Gilbert, Smith and Rosenbaum as similarly in thrall to 'l'idéal de l'ingénieur'.

In the space that remains in this article, I would like to discuss some poems by O'Hara and Guillaume Apollinaire in which walking overlaps with and is complicated by different kinds of movement leading towards a still point which ironically most recalls Delaunay's warning to the Futurists: 'Vous marchez véritablement à la mort'. The relation between the walk poetry of O'Hara and Apollinaire also reflects another transatlantic power shift, one that was asserted most explicitly by David Lehman in *The Last Avant Garde: The Making of the New York School of Poets*:

> The poets of the New York School were as heterodox, as belligerent toward the literary establishment, and as loyal to each other, as their Parisian predecessors had been. The 1950s and early 60s in New York were their banquet years. It is as though they translated the avant-garde idiom of "perpetual collaboration" from the argot of turn-of-the-century Paris to the rough hewn vernacular of the American metropolis at midcentury.[15]

Here, Lehman refers to Roger Shattuck's book *The Banquet Years* in which Apollinaire features alongside Satie, Jarry and le Douanier Rousseau as the embodiment of the Paris avant-garde. For Lehman, O'Hara was not only walking around New York: the territory of Paris, too, was surrendered to a 'rough-hewn' American avant-garde. In this context, the assertion of a naïve quality of resistance in the act of walking is rendered still more problematic.

In 'Zone' and 'Le musicien de Saint-Merry', Apollinaire presents himself walking through Paris: the poet makes an appeal to a rising movement which, according to Philippe Renaud, answers 'une volonté de posséder les choses par le regard'.[16] Movement through space enables movement back through time in memory, which in turn initiates simultaneity, so that the speaker is seen to be present in different places at the same time. 'Zone' presents a walk from the centre of Paris to the suburb of Auteuil where Apollinaire lived: beginning by the Eiffel Tower in the morning, the poet goes book-shopping on the quais, admires 'la grace de cette rue industrielle', walks 'seul parmi la foule' like Baudelaire's *flâneur*, has a coffee in a bar 'parmi les malheureux', goes to a restaurant at night, and walks home as day breaks. During this walk the poet witnesses the century becoming a bird which then flies through the air 'comme Jésus', accompanied by angels and priests 'qui montent éternellement élevant l'hostie'. This 'premier aéroplane' then comes to land and the sky is filled instead with birds, real and imaginary, who have come to 'fraternise' with the 'volante machine'. We then return abruptly to walking around Paris before a series of images is initiated in which the poet appears simultaneously on the Mediterranean coast, in a garden in Prague, in Koblenz, and elsewhere: a second rising movement occurs as the poet moves backwards through his life 'En montant au Hradchin', joining temporal to spatial dominance. But the visionary access granted in the poem is marked by disruption and the recurrence of barriers: shame prevents the walker entering a church to confess, he recalls being thrown in jail, and the memory of unrequited love persists throughout the poem. As the walker returns home to sleep amid a collection of African fetishes themselves seen as rendering imperfect access to holy presence ('les Christ inférieurs des obscures espérances') he bids adieu to the sun, seen as a severed head.

'Le musicien de Saint-Merry' similarly follows the speaker's horizontal movement through the city but impedence is much more immediately registered as the poet's opening claim to the right 'de saluer des êtres que je ne connais pas' is undermined by the unavailability of those beings as they pass before the poet 'et s'accumulent au loin'. The poetic power of summoning is usurped by the 'musicien' who, playing the poet's own 'air', leads the women of Saint-Merry through the streets of the quartier to an abandoned house where they disappear. As the musician goes on his way 'terriblement', the poet registers effects of simultaneity which also frustrate his desires through the memory of unrequited love. Here, a rising movement through the city figures the poet's surrender to sameness as the world beneath becomes a vertiginous and unassimilable multiplicity:

> *Nous nous ressemblons comme dans l'architecture du siècle dernier*
> Ces hautes cheminées pareilles à des tours
> Nous allons plus haut maintenant et ne touchons plus le sol
>
> Et tandis que le monde vivait et variait

Both poems involve movements which lead to stasis: poetic 'simultaneity', the disputed terrain of Delaunay and the Futurists, is an effect of movement, forcefully registered in the anaphoric emphases of the isolated lines which convey the images of omnipresence, but which is concerned with the suppression of movement: it is ironic that those sections of the poem where transitions from one line to another are most underlined should be those where the poet asserts his transcendence of time and space. The necessity in the poem of a temporal sequence where a painting may indicate multiple possibilities within a pictorial space was apparent to Apollinaire in his art criticism.[17] In this way the sequence of the walk through the city becomes repeatedly associated thematically with the inescapable movement towards death: the severed head of the sun in 'Zone', the abandoned house and the 'flute lointaine' which makes a dying sound at the end of 'Le musicien de Saint-Merry'.[18]

In Frank O'Hara's poetry, the bohemian *flâneur* of Apollinaire's Paris is replaced by the figure of the white-collar worker who must find the time to walk or to write according to the dictates of the everyday working schedule: thus, O'Hara claimed to have composed his *Lunch Poems* in 'the noisy splintered glare of a Manhattan noon' on his lunch hour. But if the *flâneur* is gone, the city of Paris remains. In 'Day and Night in 1952', O'Hara writes:

> Of
> distances I can only say Paris! you of
> the paper route, you fictitious of
> all the prancers in my ardent imagination of
> which are you not the least and most of
> what I think about the world of
> no illusion, not an iota!

Again and again this city 'prances' through O'Hara's ardent imagination: in 'Second Avenue' we have 'a Paris / of voluptuary chases, lays, choices, what we know and savor'; in 'Adieu to Norman, Bon Jour [sic] to Joan and Jean-Paul', O'Hara contemplates the rue Frémicourt on a map of Paris and is 'happy to find it like a bird / flying over Paris et ses environs'. He exclaims: 'I wish I were reeling around Paris / instead of reeling around New York' and the willed, continuous presence of the poet's friends, Allen, Peter, and the recently married Jane Hazan, née Freilicher (whose absence so often troubles him), becomes synonymous with the willed continuous presence of an avant-garde in New York to match that of Paris and, indeed, the continuous presence of the poem in time:

> the only thing to do is simply continue
> [...]
> blue light over the Bois de Boulogne it continues
> the Seine continues
> the Louvre stays open it hardly closes at all
> [...]
> Shirley Goldfarb continues to be Shirley Goldfarb
> and Jane Hazan continues to be Jane Freilicher (I think!)
> [...]
> but we shall continue to be ourselves everything continues to
>   be possible
> René Char, Pierre Reverdy, Samuel Beckett it is possible isn't it
> I love Reverdy for saying yes, though I don't believe it

The variousness of movement, the spatial and temporal anxieties and the recourse to simultaneity we have observed in Apollinaire's poetry are all present in 'Adieu to Norman...'. But it is in 'Rhapsody' that O'Hara's affinity with Apollinaire's walk poems is most striking. In 'Rhapsody', the New York pedestrian pauses before the door of 515 Madison Avenue, the 'portal / stopped realities' of which seem to offer access to an eroticised space characterised by dizzying vertical motion: 'your marble is bronze and your lianas elevator cables / swinging from the myth of ascending'. Falling, and failing ('declining the challenge of racial attractions'), frustrated desire seeks its fulfilment instead in a celebration which extends down and out and into simultaneity through the 'midtown tunnels and the tunnels, too, of Holland'. 'Une volonté de posséder les choses par le regard' is signalled in the poet's renewed search for 'the summit where all aims are clear' but O'Hara mocks the upward impulses of civic ambition as they coincide with his own:

> a sight of Manahatta in the towering needle
> multi-faceted insight of the fly in the stringless labyrinth
> Canada plans a higher place than the Empire State Building

Conversation with a cab driver seems to offer the chance to salute beings that the poet does not know, but even in the company of the serene image of the lover ('you were there always and you know all about these things') it is the obscure threat of 'the gauntlet' which comes to predominate, so that movement through the city is associated with violence and rejection, initiating a menacing simultaneity whereby an allusion to the Chinese repression of a Tibetan uprising coincides with the poet's own oath of allegiance to 'the enormous bliss of American death' as he sits sorting his poems.

This represents the culmination of O'Hara's engagement with Apollinaire and the Paris avant-garde. Here, the anxieties about desire and death which impel the figures who walk through Paris and New York are made to coincide with the territorial ambitions of nation states. All the resources of movement which are brought to bear in an attempt to constitute the dynamic and extensive figure of the poet in an urban landscape in fact result in the establishment of a territory which replaces and absorbs that figure back into itself. Inevitably, gait technology comes to identify not only people but also the space across which they walk.

Notes

1. Rimbaud, *Poésies, Une saison en enfer, Illuminations*, ed. by Louis Forestier (Paris: Éditions Gallimard, 1973; repr. 1993), p. 175.
2. Robert Delaunay, quoted in Timothy Mathews, *Reading Apollinaire : theories of poetic language* (Manchester: Manchester University Press, 1987), pp. 114–115.
3. Roger Gilbert, *Walks in the World: Representation and Experience in Modern American Poetry* (Princeton: Princeton University Press, 1991), p. 3.
4. Gilbert, ibid., p. 45.
5. Gilbert, ibid., p. 48.
6. Anne D. Wallace, *Walking, Literature, and English Culture: The Origins and Uses of Peripatetic in the Nineteenth Century* (Oxford: Clarendon Press, 1993), p. 15.
7. Harold Rosenberg, *The Tradition of the New* (Chicago: The University of Chicago Press, 1960; repr. 1982), p. 14.
8. Michel de Certeau, *L'invention du quotidien: 1. arts de faire* (Paris: Éditions Gallimard, 1990), p. 142.
9. de Certeau, *L'invention du quotidien*, p. 141
10. de Certeau, ibid., pp. 59–60
11. de Certeau, ibid., p. 153.
12. For a discussion of 're-employments', see Jeremy Ahearne, *Michel de Certeau: Interpretation and its Other* (Cambridge: Polity Press, 1995), pp. 29–33. De Certeau's writing on walking is illuminated on pp. 176–182, where Ahearne insists: 'this second, poetic geography is not a reductively aestheticized or ethereal construct. It represents rather a 'practical' geography in so far as it is a product of the ways in which inhabitants actually put their environments 'into practice' [...] de Certeau works with a notion of *poeisis* which is inseparable from the realm of everyday social exchanges, ties and constraints, and which displaces the more narrowly literary affiliations of the term.' (p. 182).
13. See 'Privacy villain of the week: DARPA's gait surveillance tech' at http://www.politechbot.com/p-04102.html
14. Mathews, *Reading Apollinaire*, p. 114
15. David Lehman, *The Last Avant Garde: The Making of the New York School of Poets* (New York: Doubleday, 1998), p. 2.
16. Philippe Renaud, *Lecture d'Apollinaire* (Lausanne: Éditions L'Age d'Homme, 1969), p. 149.
17. See Mathews, *Reading Apollinaire*, pp. 86–125, for an account of this.
18. See Renaud, *Lecture d'Apollinaire*, pp. 148–149, for a discussion of this tendency in a wider context in Apollinaire's work.

Four Walking Pieces

PETER RILEY

Walking

I remember what it was like, walking across the land,
The long roads you covered for days with
Nothing to hear but birds and trees, occasional
Tractors ploughing the land and the wind blowing
Kind or cruel as the wind blows and sometimes
It rained and you got soaked as you walked in those
Old macks that absorb water but chances were
You walked on in the wind and dried out before
You stopped for the night, you stopped at inns
Or in good weather lay under a hedge to rouse
At dawn as the sharp faint light spread sideways
Across the fields droplets gleaming on the leaves
And ate your bread and cheese for breakfast and
Shat behind a tree and walked on over the next
Hill along the next valley for the next day or
Over the plains between the wheat fields from
Village to village crossing rivers by bridges
And fords, no special equipment needed you just
Put on your mack and grabbed a little rucksack
And walked out of your house to get a bus or
Train to somewhere you could walk, on the paths or
Roads as you needed to, not many vehicles around,
Quiet landscapes, but there used to be a lot of
Bird song in the air in those days and when
You got to villages they were usually busy specially
At weekends and after school when the children
Were playing and shouting on the green, these days
The villages and fields everywhere are silent but for
A constant slight grumbling from the sky you could
Buy food from houses and farms, you lived off

Pieces of bread, cheese, apples, chocolate and
Evening dinners at pubs it was a very good way of
Enjoying yourself on a small income you could
Do it for two or three weeks at a run whenever
You were free though spring and autumn were best
And my word how you could think on those walks!
The mind free of avoidance and resentment ambled
Far off on its own in logical steps and sudden leaps
Like someone clearing a stream as you walked on
Hearing and seeing everything and you nodded
To the people you passed, dwellers in farms villages and
Small towns who were, what shall I say, locals
In a way they no longer are, well they were likely
To speak to you given a chance they were
Always interested in someone from somewhere else
You didn't want to buy their homes and they
Weren't going to talk television but you'd follow
Together the graceful discourses and gentle hopes
Of early socialism in a friendly sparring match
Between news of wars and horses, as you drank
The fresh ale in a village inn to end the day
Alone swaying up wooden stairs to a room with a small
Wood fire in the grate and a window under the eaves
Opening onto total blackness and silence, the
Country night in its usual persistent force.
I remember doing this out of sheer pleasure and a sense
Of partaking of breadth, but also persistently
Grasping an opportunity, as if it were bound to end.

Journal Entry

Sunday. There is an open shop, and welcoming person: "It's a friendly village ..." Bread, tomatoes, and some very fine Stilton. Set off westwards though the village. The singing chapel, standing beside the road like a stone transistor radio, emanating harmony. Muddy path over mine mounds towards Long Rake, and over the top pastures. One remaining tumulus, Calling Low, hidden in the woods to the right. A small pond of liquid mud and cow dung completely filling a gateway. Stonewall mountaineering. Sloping grass fields perilously slippery in places. The steps down into Cales Dale, taken very carefully. A jay below, gliding up the dale, perfect speed neither early nor late. Like the Methodists, in perfect time. Down to Lathkill, over the spring and left upstream to the head cave. Eat an apple. People passing by always stop here, whether it's lunch time or not, and gaze at a volume of water issuing from a cave mouth in the valley side, suspending thought of good and bad or what comes next, happy to be reminded that the earth continues. Death is kind. Strong flow today, though it hasn't rained. A man with a small dog's head peering out of his rucksack. Walk back downstream, quietly singing improvised hymns to myself, because you should sing, and people used to sing. Death is suspect, and needs persuading. Tough walking on stones, the path gets involved with the river. Left boot lets in water on front edge of upper. The day thou gavest. Though it's hardly started yet. Into the private sector, barbed wire, walking by permission, otherwise similar. River overtakes on the right. Walking much easier now, so that vacant hollows form in the mind. What shall I do with them? Leave the valley and climb up to Over Haddon, last seen circa 1956 and gone dead: no pub, no shop, half the houses Peak-Parked so they look like public toilets. That's wealth. Return to the valley, on down lower Lathkill. Vacant hollows throbbing. A few people about. Companionship of the old and the very young, travelling across all those years in an instant, a no-time which is unconstructable. Trout jumping waterfall: the energy thrust and impetus needed to stay where you are. Hollows contracting. A grey wagtail at Conksbury Bridge. Road back to Youlgrave slow in the rain. Big notice for Countryside Alliance stuck on a barn: "It's worth fighting for." Vaguely disgruntled privilege parading as militancy. Left and right, blame disguised as praise. But love creates no outsiders. TRUE LOVE CREATES NO OUTSIDERS! I don't know anything about death but that's what it is about love. So I found something to do with one of the brain bubbles. A receptacle. The truth calling low over the hilltops. And onto the High Street again, still raining, seeking oatcakes (the floppy kind). No oatcakes! Oatcakes finished: EEC regulations concerning the bleaching of flour. That's progress. Dinner alone at the house and the day ends. Village night silence, with the river muttering below and a few owls in its trees, but still a silence, a specific silence. Maniac hammering on the door at 6 a.m. and screaming about a parked car.

Alpine Zones: The Reward

Why do we come here, hurt ourselves, strain body and mind to the edge of endurance? The valley of a thousand streams. The impossibility of the place. A thousand streams up there, a thousand quagmires down here.

The thin waterfalls high up the slopes, misty, incessant, aged presences. The streams trailing down the valley sides as raggedy white lines, which when you get up to them are substantial torrents, crossed with great difficulty, leaping with yells onto tufts and wet rocks. The Chinese aspect is half way to the sky.

The river divided into three above Peyregrand on the valley floor, rattling over the stones, waded with ease but icy cold. Three times we stand on the edge and fling as hard as we can two pairs of boots, and a large rolled umbrella, over to the other side.

Many azalea bushes with small, rose-like, deep red flowers, all over the hillsides among the rocks and boulders.

Big patches of dog's-tooth violet mixed in with the grasses. I zip open the tent flap in the morning and find my nose touching one.

Occasional wild tulips, all closed, red-yellow streaks emerging from the ends of stems. Then suddenly three of them beside the path wide open: big six-pointed yellow stars.

Three kinds of gentian, which Lawrence wrote as "burning dark blue / giving off blue darkness" — the miniature, the normal, and the attenuated or "trumpet gentian" (is this official terminology?) At wild heights, deep blue flames among wiry grass.

Hellebore in great quantity, mostly not yet in flower, lush clusters of ridged leaves close to water.

If you attempt to sit on the hillside the wiry sharp-pointed brown grass penetrates your clothing and pricks you.

The snow-melt late this year. High up, big patches of snow still remaining, perilous uncertainties across the paths, upper surfaces crusted and pitted, sometimes concealing quite big streams, which you can hear passing under the snow.

Insofar as there are paths in the uppermost zones — small piles of stones on the tops of boulders.

Mountain pastures crowded with orchids, mostly purple but also yellow, and orchid-like flowers, among which an unidentified sort of miniature turret of red cabbage.

Crowds of hyacinth, and yellow daffodils, and the "narcissus-flowered anemone", and the smaller daffodil, "the poet's narcissus", white with slight yellow trumpet. Dozens of them at a time.

Alpine zones in late spring. Snow-melt, swollen streams, a million small flowers. Small everything: small butterflies, small moths, small ants. Small junipers. Wire grass like needles. Small birds, a few. Small ripples over the whole surface of the lake, deep green. Cirrus on deep blue.

How the flower species seem to accommodate themselves to the available terrain, as if not in competition. A richness not dependent on an elsewhere. The result no doubt of a great deal of diplomacy.

An iridescent turquoise beetle minding its business on a grass stalk. A minute moth exactly the appearance of a petal of speedwell. Pastel blue with white border.

But where are the birds? This is lammergaier land, where are they? And the vultures and the eagles? In two weeks all we get one raven at Tristaina and a raptor disappearing into a fir tree near Siguer. And small greyish fluffy things darting over the snow so fast you can't see them, emitting a noise like a telephone ringing.

A little thunder as a bank of snow detaches itself and falls into the lake.

Why is the lake called "Tristaina"?

However high up you get, through whatever steep declivities and rocky paths of agonising demand across and over massive geological barriers from shelf to shelf many hundreds of metres into the sky — the animals and their herders have been there before you, the dung on the ground, this year's or last.

And no flies. Instead: dung-beetles, small black shiny creatures in clusters, crawling around and flying, which never seek to interfere with you.

The continuous sound of falling water, wherever you go. Wherever you sleep.

It hurts the body to move. It hurts the mind to fail. It hurts the spirit to contemplate the economic and social condition of the Principality of Andorra.

Never an easeful step. Where to put the foot, always a problem to be solved, even downhill at some speed. Rock edges and water routes share the pavement. A mediaeval muleteers' track, in some parts supported by quite massive masonry built up against the wall of cliff or canyon, in other parts vanished without trace, dispersed into bog and bilberry pits, leaving you to cross a torrent as best you can.

The main road becomes the illicit route. From France to Spain by the Port de Siguer through Andorra, trod no doubt by merchant caravans, troubadours, wide ranging shepherds, and later by Cathars, a precious book held under the arm, the only copy... and Cathar persecutors. A muleteers' route, a smugglers' route, an escape route for Jews and resistance during the German occupation, a group of which intercepted at Siguer village in 1943 and executed by shooting against a wall on the north edge of the village. There is a plaque.

Finally lakes. Mountain-top lakes nested in cirques, great cliffs plunging into them or maybe one side melting out into pasture. Clear or choked, but the only flat things within 20 kilometres. Bent lakes following the valley curve, or placid almost square lakes in the tops surrounded by snowy crests. The surface covered in small ripples, the water absolutely clear, very cold, with, when drunk, the metallic taste of recently melted snow. And water falling from these lakes over shallow ledges to trail down the valleys accumulating more and more substance from side streams ... Always the sound of falling water wherever you go and whatever you do, wake or sleep or walk or toil, stand still or lie down to rest, alongside the sound of falling water.

And at night the star dome, magnified and clarified in the great cut above the valley sides. All the rustling water on the deep grey sloping earth, and up there they stand silent on pure black distance a crowd, a crown, a vast donation, the reward.

Why we come here. Two people walking down a small road in the Pyrenees in gentle rain under a large red and white striped umbrella from Asda as the daylight dims. No other reason. A song-like reason.

How To Get To Ágios Pantaleímon At Boularií

When you reach a modern Church, the Dormition, you're in the upper village though there aren't any houses to be seen, just a few stone towers higher up the hill. Walk on up the road, which crosses a stream, and look for a small rock outcrop to the left before the white wall of a smallholding. This is the beginning of an old mule track which continues beside the wall, then meets another track from the right and goes on in the same direction beyond the village, following the contour of the hillside, running between low stone walls. It's a little used track and stones from the walls have fallen into it making a difficult floor for the foot in many places, and vegetation has sprung up from the dry brown earth, most of it bearing points and spikes: small thorn bushes and ilex, various thistles with purple or yellow flowers, bramble-like plants that trap your legs and can trip you up and scratch you at the same time. You need quite heavy trousers but some of those spikes are so strong they will get through denim, particularly those of a pretty yellow thistle bearing a round daisy-like flower with a cross of four long points behind its head, on the end of a bending stem. There is also a small spiked seed-pod which has a habit of getting inside shoes and a thunderbolt-like feature of conjoined stalks which detaches itself from one of these plants and by a band of barbed Velcro-like surface fastens itself persistently to any textile, especially exposed areas of socks, and is difficult to pull off. These enemies are not dense on the path but you are rarely free of them. After 500m there is a small ruined church on the right made of big stones, which a collapsed roof makes it impossible to enter.

Here the route departs from the track which just seems to disappear and you are among old disused olive terraces. The only path through them consists of that made by the very few people who make their way to St Pantaleímon, so you watch carefully for worn ground surface and gaps in vegetation, continuing ahead but slightly to the left of the terrace courses. That is, keep straight ahead but tend left. Go straight forwards, but think left, or allow left to happen as by a slight gravitation. Watch particularly for the blaze of deep red soil each time the route cuts to the next terrace down, only a metre or so deep. Look ahead, but thinking right, for the glimpse of a small roof of long stones among the trees about 100m away, and when you see it tend slightly to the left of its direction and you should enter a small enclosure of very old olives among white rocks, and then advance towards the church.

It looks like an old stone hovel, sheep shelter, cowshed, with the slight but tell-tale projection of the apses at the east end with their own fanning slab roof. The whole thing is no more than 20m long with a roof over half of it. You can get in by where the north door used to be, a gap in the wall with a wooden pallet placed across it held in place by an upright stone slab (replace these when you leave), into the west end which has collapsed completely and is open to the sky. But the east end is still intact, like a cave in a series of three arches before you, with the ruined iconostasis wall coming in from both sides at the last arch to mark off the curved space at the end. The wall surfaces from the first arch on still bear frescoes, at first fragmentarily among damage but increasingly intact as you get to the east end. They have been dated by an inscription to the ninth Century.

Keep on walking. The two great martyrs stare out at you from the two apse alcoves with both hands raised, *orant*, their heads crushed into the arching roofs of their spaces. Pantaleímon to the north, Nicetas to the south, old-blood red robes, ochre for skin, white marks for ornament, what survives as blue-grey-to-brown for hair and bodice. Pantaleímon, a doctor of Nicomedia who after being Christianised stopped charging for his services, martyred c.300. Relics of his blood kept at Constantinople, Ravello, and Madrid miraculously liquefy on his feast day. Nicetas, bishop of Remeciana east of the Danube in what is now Romania: a Goth, believed by some to be the author of the Te Deum, killed c370 in the persecutions of Athamarian. These completely dominate the figuration, there is no space for the Virgin between them and she is set centrally in a lumpy band above their heads. On the north sanctuary wall is an odd picture of the bathing of the holy infant, the body immersed in a kind of grey horse-shoe and the haloed head of a man of about 50 looking rather indignant above it. This is opposite the baptism on the south wall, and these are what remain of a cycle of the life of Christ which would have filled the church walls. Keep on walking. Push through the thistles and briars. On the south wall outside the sanctuary is a remarkably well preserved figure of St Cyriaca, another Nicomedian martyr, one of six maidens who died at the stake in 307. But a different martyrdom, a later fresco in a different style, with a more sophisticated regular patterning of ornamentation superimposed on the robes. A smooth, a forgotten death, and a large wasps' nest above where the wall meets the roof. Go back to the east end. Broad red lines on white, blue brown and black patches filling the outlines, rough-cut jewels of paint. Two martyrs. Look straight at them but think round them. Push past the enemies, the attractiveness, the foreignness, the remoteness. Look at the big serious faces, the raised hands, denying access. Speaking of fanaticism and a kind of love, speaking of focus and the self tunnelled into its purpose, to the point of suicession. Where the self ends itself, for the sake of a future, an unknowable. And what survives, in the profession of doctor, the history of concern, from these far distant lives, what seeds of extreme distance still stick to us. The two big pairs of eyes looking back at you, wide open, full of death. This is what you came here for.

Author's Note.

Walking was written in 1991. The imaginary country it constructs was drawn from a variety of directly experienced and reported places all over the world, the latter mostly dated in the first half of the twentieth century. The other three pieces are accurate reports of walks undertaken in 2002, 2004 and 2005.

Freeing the Waters—Poetry in a Parched Culture

MICHAEL SYMMONS ROBERTS

In the notes to his epic poem *The Anathemata*, the great Anglo-Welsh modernist David Jones describes a memory that fed his imagination. Thirty-five years before publishing *The Anathemata* in 1952, he was staying in Wales, at Capel y Ffin. On Christmas Eve, the water supply to the house suddenly ran dry, and Jones and the writer Rene Hague set off to find the source of the mountain-stream which gave the house its water. Right at the source, they found that the stream had been deliberately blocked and diverted, so they *freed the waters*, and followed those waters back to Capel y Ffin for Christmas Day. This image of 'freeing the waters' continued to resonate with Jones, and recurs in his work. It comes in *The Anathemata* as part of a passage rich in water metaphors, full of rivers and fountains and oceans, a passage which culminates in Christ's cry from the cross, as set down in the Good Friday liturgy—'Sitio'—'I thirst'. In the preface to this epic poem, Jones writes

> Water is called the *matter* of the Sacrament of Baptism. Is two of hydrogen and one of oxygen that *matter*? I suppose so. But a knowledge of the chemical components of this material water should, normally, or if you prefer it, ideally, provide us with further, deeper, and more exciting significances vis-à-vis the sacrament of water, and also, for us islanders, whose history is so much of water, with other significances relative to that.

David Jones believed that the artist, the poet, should be a maker of signs. But writing in 1951, he warned of a growing crisis facing poetry—a crisis of dead or dying signs and symbols. Using the example of the word 'wood'—although it could just as easily be applied to blood, or water—he said

> If the poet writes *wood*, what are the chances that the Wood of the Cross will be evoked? Should the answer

be 'None', then it would seem that an impoverishment of some sort would have to be admitted. It would mean that that particular word could no longer be used with confidence to implement, to call up or to set in motion a whole world of content belonging in a special sense to the mythus of a particular culture and of concepts and realities belonging to mankind as such. This would be true irrespective of our beliefs or disbeliefs. It would remain true even if we were of the opinion that it was high time that the word *wood* should be dissociated from the mythus and concepts indicated. The arts abhor any loppings off of meanings or emptyings out, any lessening of the totality of connotation, and loss of recession and thickness through.

Perhaps Jones' words were less of a warning, and more of a lament. Once it begins, no poet or educator or politician can stop what Seamus Heaney has called 'the big lightening, the emptying out' of our religious language. In *The Triumph of Love*, Geoffrey Hill writes of England as 'a nation with so many memorials but no memory.' Could the same be said of the English language itself?

In the face of this, one might expect poets to be freeing the waters, to be refreshing and reviving the very language they use. Some are, but many others at the cutting edge of poetic writing and criticism rejoice in throwing off the baggage of sign-making and truth-seeking. An editorial in *Poetry Review* on the legacy of modernism spoke of one of its lasting effects as 'an embargo on the windy abstractions much loved by the 19th Century', and goes on to assert that 'practically all serious poets are still modernists in this sense'. As a warning against religiosity and portentousness, and a yearning for poets to make their ideas concrete, that's fair enough, and pretty much all serious poets would go along with it. But if, as I suspect, words like 'God', 'soul' and 'grace' would be on the list of windy abstractions, then a presumed embargo on those words could be seen as a presumed embargo on many kinds of religious or metaphysical poetry.

If the language of poetry has become *parched* in our culture, *parched* of truth or meaning beyond the poem itself, parched of historical associations and resonances, parched of its potential to hold up, as David Jones would see it, 'valid signs', then this is a particular crisis for religious poetry. T. S. Eliot famously said of William Blake that since he worked within no tradition, he had to invent a religion and world view as well as to write original poetry. Eliot disapproved of this, believing that innovation was best confined to the poetry, and that that aim was best achieved by writing within a solid framework, which for him was Anglo-Catholic, Conservative and Royalist, but could equally be Protestant Nonconformist, politically radical and republican—closer to Basil Bunting's framework. But in a parched poetic culture, how can the metaphysical, the theological, the mystical be expressed or even approached? The most widely acceptable term at the moment seems to be 'spiritual'. Poetry can be 'spiritual' without being seen as 'religious'. Indeed, many would argue that *all* poetry is or should be spiritual. What is 'Spiritual poetry'?

The composer James MacMillan—with whom I have been working as a librettist and collaborator for over a decade—has written about the current dominance of 'spiritual' music on the classical scene. He is often grouped with John Tavener, Henryk Górecki, and Arvo Pärt—all overtly Christian composers, all commissioned and performed by orchestras across the world, all at the height of their reputation. Does this mean that music is less hostile to the 'religious' than poetry? Less parched even? Well, it doesn't take much listening to John Tavener's music to realise that his central vision, the icon of his music, if you like, is that of Christ risen, ascended, glorified. Tavener, like Pärt and Górecki, has in his music explicitly turned his back on conflict, drama, suffering, and fallenness. One of the most striking aspects of James MacMillan's music is that the whole story is there, the whole drama. Christ could not have risen if he had not been crucified first. The battle is ultimately won, but it continues all around us. Truly religious art, truly Christian art—whether music or poetry—must surely live and draw creative breath from that tension, that struggle, that completeness in the midst of incompleteness. 'Spiritual' music, like 'spiritual' poetry, has come to mean a kind of one-dimensional heightened or transcendent experience without any sense of sacrifice or conflict. Even though it is often very accomplished and very beautiful, it has come to mean a flight from reality, an escape from the darkness. T.S. Eliot wrote that 'For the great majority of people who love poetry, 'religious' poetry is a variety of minor poetry: the religious poet is not a poet who is treating the whole subject of poetry in a religious spirit, but [...] is leaving out what men consider their major passions, and thereby confessing to his ignorance of them.' Perhaps some of the rather thin art produced in recent years under the banner 'spiritual' deserves to be regarded as 'minor' work. But here I'm returning to the central question, to use Eliot's definition— how can a contemporary poet 'treat the whole subject of poetry in a religious spirit?'

The philosopher John Millbank argues that 'Poetry is not fiction, but the most intense of real interventions.' He elaborates that

> Of its essence, poetry makes, but it makes only to see further, and to establish something real in the world: real, because it further manifests the ideal and abiding. In this context it can be seen that its unavoidable detour via fiction is paradoxically a sign of its necessary humility: it must, in part, conjecture, since it cannot fully see and create in one simple intuition, like God himself.

I'm presuming that he means good poetry, or real poetry, or poetry that works. To borrow a word from another philosopher, Catherine Pickstock, I've begun to see poems—and that movement or dynamic within poems—as 'liturgies'. Pickstock uses the word liturgy to analyse our secular culture. She argues that secularism is not built on reason (as is often claimed), but is sustained by myths and rituals which alone secure a substantive emptiness. Just as there were once all-encompassing daily rituals which inculcated a sense of transcendence, so now there are equally all-encompassing rituals which inculcate a sense of a world without mystery, closed in upon itself. Thus, for Pickstock, the central task of philosophical theology becomes one of exposing and decoding these secular myths and rituals. Poems are ritualistic, not read like most prose to follow a story or glean information, poetry is incantatory, thrives on repetition, and is best learnt by heart. If, in this sense, poems too are liturgies, or parts of greater liturgies, then they can be liturgies of profundity, truth and meaning, or empty liturgies. Our choice is not between a seemingly narrow religious poetry or a postmodern writing free from cultural constraints and assumptions. Our choice is which liturgies we choose.

The Australian poet Les Murray has spoken of the defining characteristic of real, whole poetry as 'presence'. Perhaps this is another way of describing John Millbank's 'something real in the world, a further manifestation of the ideal and abiding.' For Murray, as for Millbank, this reality, this presence, is fundamentally Christian. For Murray in particular, it has a sacramental sense, as a Catholic poet who believes in the real presence at the heart of the Mass. But if real, true great poems are 'epiphanies'—a word now regularly used by secular critics to describe what poems can do—then they need to be hard earned epiphanies.

David Jones, who had so acutely described the crisis of religious language in poetry almost half a century ago, did attempt to mark out a way forward too. As a poet, it was natural for him to look for this way forward by burrowing deep into the roots of the language itself. In an essay called 'Art and Sacrament', he said

> I understand that more than one opinion has prevailed with regard to the etymology of the word *religio*, but a commonly accepted view is that a binding of some sort is indicated. The same root is in 'ligament', a binding that supports an organ and assures that organ its freedom of use as part of a body. And it is in this sense that I here use the word 'religious'. It refers to a binding, a securing. Like the ligament, it secures a freedom to function. The binding makes possible the freedom. Cut the ligament and there is atrophy— corpse rather than corpus. If this is true, then the word religion makes no sense unless we presuppose a freedom of some sort.

So perhaps to 'free the waters' and help slake the thirst of a parched culture, poets and other artists *need* religion, *need* a theology. Now there's an unfashionable idea. There's a popular view, influenced by Romanticism, that only the pure, unfettered imagination can produce the great work. Poets should not be religious, or overtly political, or committed to anything much outside the poetry. Poets should be freewheeling, freethinking free spirits. As if that meant anything. It chimes with James MacMillan's experience of fellow composers feeling that music is complete in itself, and shouldn't be sullied by any extra-musical element. It is all about 'the dots on the page'. Well, if David Jones is right, then that image of the free-spirited artist is, and always has been, an illusion. Freedom is not absence. The binding makes possible the freedom. We are all engaged in liturgies, but those liturgies can be empty or profound. Poets can choose, can and should create and recreate. They should kick, rebel, challenge and question, but they cannot opt out. When I think of Jones' 'binding to make free', I think of a composer like Olivier Messiaen, whose technical and imaginative virtuosity underlie much of contemporary classical music—inspiring pupils such as Pierre Boulez. But Messiaen is a problem for the likes of Boulez, because his expansive creativity arose out of a very orthodox Catholic Christianity. Post-modernist music critics try to cope with Messiaen by separating his music from his faith, which they regard as a bizarre personal idiosyncrasy. The Welsh poet Waldo Williams described his religion and his native language (he believed the two to be inextricably linked) as 'a large room within narrow walls.' In other words, as with Messiaen, it was a radical freedom won through constraint, a 'binding to make free.'

And if religious poetry is a radical and liberating act, then how much more radical, and how much more liberating is praise poetry. Those religious poets in the late 20th Century who found praise hard to write—including great religious poets like the English Geoffrey Hill and the American John Berryman—have still found material in the often frustrated desire to praise. The leading Welsh language poet writing today—Bobi Jones—is a convert to that language from a Cardiff English-speaking family. He is also a convert to Calvinism. Both put him in the margins of contemporary western culture, yet he has written a substantial body of work that makes clear his commitment to praise. In his own words : 'Praise continues, even at the deepest level, but it is praise under siege.' In this he is by no means alone in Wales, but the comparison with a literary tradition so close geographically, yet so utterly foreign to English has a particular bearing on praise poetry.

In Bobi Jones' case, praise is not so much a choice as a religious duty. As a Calvinist, the cultural mandate given to man by God in Genesis, emphasises man's purposeful activity on earth, to replenish and fructify it, but above all to praise, serve and enjoy God forever. That a contemporary poet might try to fulfil such a commandment is, depending on your personal beliefs, either crazy or revolutionary. It is certainly no longer a conformist choice. Bobi Jones himself, writing about his formation as a poet, has written about the society around him, and the choices he faced:

> Obviously, the aimlessness could not just be avoided: one could not flee the wilful incomprehensibility or the brainwashing onslaught on order and significant conceptualising: one could not just dump the ironic destruction of family life, the agnostic hatred of Welsh identity, and the whole artistic attempt to reflect or interpret this absurd world with over-modest fidelity. One could not go back. Indeed, my own work was something of an interpretation, but it was also an attempt to free itself without 'escape'. It was a deliberate re-orientation.

'Freedom without escape', a binding to make free.

Praise poetry is radical for a number of reasons. It is radical because is it is hard to write with authenticity, especially in a language so emptied of religious significance as English. It is radical because it is realistic. It is not optimistic, but as Bobi Jones expresses it, 'praise is the completest refusal I know of the absurd. And it unashamedly and pointedly has a direction.' Commenting on the plight of the religious poet writing in English, as compared to his own Welsh, Bobi Jones picked up on the 'fashionable dryness, which has not always been part of the tradition, and can be almost neurotic.' But he added that 'A dry ironic spell should not necessarily be a bad thing, as long as praise is not permanently inhibited, and as long as poets are permitted once more to stand on their heads.'

My own experience as a poet is that authentic praise is the note I find hardest to strike. I do believe in its radicalism, and in its power when it can be achieved. But writing in English, in a poetic tradition so smashed and uprooted, I have so far not been satisfied with my own attempts at praise. It has crept up on me at times, in poems which were not intended to attempt praise, and I've been surprised to find that note struck as I look back at some of my work. But more often than not, I find as the theologian, poet and Archbishop Rowan Williams has said, that 'the attempt to mend the fracture brings about another fracture'.

Even that fracture can be fruitful though. In a recent lecture, Rowan Williams spoke about two possible strategies by which contemporary poets can write religious poetry. The first is—as many poets have attempted—to try to think or feel yourself into someone else's religious sensibility. The second, and to me the most fascinating and most frequently experienced, is the attempt to write into and around the gaps, the fractures, the silence. This will be a religious poetry in which the breakages and shortfalls of the language are significant. They will not always, indeed perhaps rarely, be about religious subject matter, but they will be written in an awareness of silence and tension. As Rowan Williams puts it : 'The articulation of that tension reveals the gap, the pulse, the rhythm.'

So, is David Jones' image of walking to the source of that stream above Capel y Ffin to free the waters still a resonant one half a century on? I think so, not least because however parched our culture might become, there is still water in abundance. The stream has been diverted—perhaps wilfully—but it has not dried up.

Works Cited

Catherine Pickstock: *After Writing* (Oxford: Blackwell Publishing, 1998)
Seamus Heaney: interview with MSR for BBC Radio 3, 1995
Geoffrey Hill: *The Triumph of Love* (London & New York: Penguin Books, 1999)
Bobi Jones: interview with MSR for BBC Radio 3, 1995
David Jones: *The Anathemata* (London: Faber, 1952)
John Millbank: letter to MSR, 1998
Les Murray: interview with MSR for BBC Radio 3, 1995
Rowan Williams: open lecture at Manchester University, 2000

W.S. Graham and the Poetics of Loss

Josh Robinson

Elegy makes more urgent the question raised by much lyric poetry: how to go about speaking to an absent addressee. Is elegy qualitatively different from other manners of lyric address, or is it a particular form of apostrophe? Does the object of elegiac address, defined to a great extent by her inability to acknowledge and respond to what is being said, differ from the addressee of other poems? W.S. Graham's poetry repeatedly poses the question of the status of the second-person pronoun, which even when presented as endowed with the capacity of speech, remains silent.[1] As Tony Lopez argues,

> There is no doubt who is speaking. The voice is always Graham's, but his position shifts in relation to his material. The person to whom he is speaking (the reader, a close friend, a lover) is always unstable.[2]

The you-figure is a mask, a persona through which no sound is able to pass, an addressee whose silence constitutes a refusal to tell us anything about his or her identity, even when named as the figure of a specific individual. This 'you' occupies an uncertain and changing position between reader, specific addressee, and indefinite pronoun.

'The Constructed Space' (161–162) recognises the difficulty of pinning down his addressee, setting out the importance of finding 'something to say [...] between us two whoever / We are'. The first person plural pronoun collapses the identity of the addressee into that of the speaking subject. The addressee is only given her own pronoun and articulated as a person in her own right in the final line of the poem's second stanza: 'And yet I say / This silence here for in it I might hear you.' This 'you' is apparently endowed with the capacity of speech, but only enters the poem as a grammatical object, someone to be heard by the poem's speaker. If the space is constructed by the act of the speaker's articulation, the silence referred to cannot exist within a lyric in which the 'you' is never given a chance to speak. Indeed, for the remainder of the poem the addressee is subsumed into the plural 'we'.

Moreover, it is not certain whether the space with which this poem is concerned is constructed by the agency of poem's speaker alone ('I [...] construct this space') or, as it is described earlier in the poem, a perhaps more communal 'space we make'.

The poem recognises that this 'constructed space' is 'a public space' in the sense not only that anyone can observe it but also that it exists between the speaker and any potential addressee (and in the case of this poem, any reader). However, no addressee is free to speak within it. Only the 'I' can 'say this silence' and thus 'this abstract act become'. In order to speak, the 'you' must itself become an 'I'. And yet the 'I' is presented as just as much a recipient as anyone else of the 'something' that 'may move across / The caught habits of language to you and me'. That is, this 'something' is not the words of the speaker, but a less tangible 'intention risen up out of nothing'. The silence of the addressee and reader does not imply passivity.

If, as Graham argues, a poem 'is brought to life by the reader and takes part in the reader's change' then the words of the poem are not the sum-total of its agency.[3] Rather, the reader is instrumental in giving the poem meaning, not merely through the act of reading out the poem and hence drawing attention to its sound-patterns, internal rhyme and the vocal 'shape' of the line and stanza, but also as the site of an affective response. By becoming one boundary of the space constructed by the poem, the reader simultaneously becomes involved in the agency of its expression and signification. Or, as Graham puts it,

> The poem itself is dumb but has the power of release. Its purpose is that it can be used by the reader to find out something about himself. Words are ambiguous. He must face it that words are ambiguous, but realise that this has to do with the fundamental force of poetry and is to be used to a positive end. The poem is not a handing out of the same packet to everyone, as it is not a thrown-down heap of words for us to choose the bonniest. The poem is the replying chord to the reader. It is the reader's involuntary reply.[4]

That is, a poem's truth-content exists within the space that is constructed between the poem and the reader who plays a part in its formation and is the site of its agency. Moreover, if the poem is 'dumb', only the reader can give voice to it: her position in relation to both speaker and addressee becomes yet more complicated. The poem uses the second-person pronoun in the act of address, but its addressee cannot always be identified, and is not identical with the reader, who encounters the sign 'you' on some occasions where it refers to (or at least includes) herself, and on others where it addresses an absent or present third party.

This you-person is particularly aporetic in elegiac address to someone presented as so obviously absent. In 'Dear Bryan Wynter' (pp.258–60), Graham confronts the difficulty of making this sort of address:

> This is only a note
> To say I am aware
> You are not here. [...]

The invocation of a named addressee puts the reader or listener in the position of someone observing a personal conversation (or address, at least) in public, as if some sort of consented eavesdropping. But if the named addressee is 'not here' and cannot hear, then to whom is the poem addressed? Where is the space in which this poem exists? Is 'here' the specific geographical location referred to in the poem—the bedroom, by the window that looks out towards St Buryan's—or the location of the reader's implied vocalisation of it?

This poem's expression of grief relies on the particular locations inhabited within it. The death of the now absent addressee puts the speaker in a particular 'position', while access to his memory seems to depend on the geographical specificity of places connected with his life and movements—'your first house', the woods 'where you used to lurk'. William Watkin argues that 'cognitively, as human beings, we map our relation to death through the spatial experiences of our life'; elegy would seem to privilege the spatial over the temporal.[5] Indeed, Wynter's absence is presented as something that is experienced most pointedly when the speaker considers a particular shared movement:

> [...]   I find
> It difficult to go
> Beside Housman's star
> Lit fences without you.

Movement through (geographical) space is not presented as the most important feature of this no-longer-shared experience that involves the transposition of a 'real' experience into the constructed space of Poem 52 of *A Shropshire Lad*, but nor is it merely incidental. While Housman's solitary wanderer 'halts and hears / My soul', Graham's invocation of his literary antecedent is a means of joining together that no longer relies on private memories, instead becoming broader, grounded in a communal poetic space. Similarly with the use of particular place-names: personal specificities are mixed with geographically verifiable and visitable locations such as Zennor and St Buryan, the latter not only a village south-west of Penzance but also a single 'u' away from the first name of the poem's addressee.

Graham's elegy to Peter Lanyon 'The Thermal Stair' (163–66) plays with place names in a similar manner. The names of the Cornish mines Botallack, Levant and Ding Dong echo respectively with a subjective 'lack', the rising like a buzzard on a thermal 'updraft' 'over the jasper sea', and the 'dingdong dingdong' toll of the funeral bells in the poem's closing lines. Here the speaker's voice is a trope not only of the attempt to address a lost addressee, but also of the initial means of discovering and confronting this loss: 'I called today, Peter, and you were away'. As Love is 'imagined into words', the problem becomes that of how it might be possible to address a dead listener. Unlike the Graham who tells Wynter that 'Speaking to you and not / Knowing if you are there / Is not too difficult', his address to Lanyon seems to require a breathless climb into the sky:

> Find me a thermal to speak and soar to you from
> Over Lanyon Quoit and the circling stones standing
> High on the moor over Gurnard's Head where some
>
> Time three foxglove summers ago, you came.

As I read this almost unpunctuated four-line sentence, I find myself short of breath, unsure as to where and whether I should stop to breathe. The line-breaks refuse the possibility of an accentuated pause, as they divide first a preposition from its object, then a participle from the adverbial phrase that qualifies it, and finally the single word 'some / Time', a division which denies the possibility of any hiatus between the two tercets. In mimicking the climb of the thermal stair, the poem induces breathlessness, the physical manifestation of a familiar trope of lyric conclusion and death.

The wish to address the dead figure can only be realised in a journey that can never successfully be made, a journey that must end in the confrontation of death, either Lanyon's own in a gliding accident or the historical deaths commemorated at his namesake Lanyon Quoit. The poem confronts this difficulty: the unattainable desired position of the physical body is tied up with the impossibility of speaking with the dead. Watkin argues that 'loss is primarily about place and placement and mourning takes us into the dead's place and out the other side'.[6] His claim is that elegiac poetry is a means of moving from the expression of mourning the condition of death to that of mourning the basic conditions of life; and that through coming to terms with the absence of the now dead other, the subject begins in turn to come to terms with its own lack through the Lacanian recognition that the subject, as someone else's object of regard, is itself a lacked object.

And yet the presence of the body which exists in 'real' space and time is essential for the construction of a poetic voice; the breath on which this voice depends must originate in a physical body. As Graham argues in a letter to Wynter:

> I remember that always somewhere under the live and speaking idiom of the Voice in poetry there is the count, the beats you can count on your fingers. Yes always under the shout and whimper and the quick and the slow of poetry there is the formal construction of time made abstract in the mind's ear. And the strange thing is that that very abstract dimension in the poem is what creates the reader's release into the human world of another.[7]

136

That is, the 'abstract' 'formal construction of time' is a means not of allowing the poet or speaker a means of communion with a lost other, but of bringing the reader (and not necessarily the addressee) into the constructed space. In 'The Thermal Stair' this is brought about first by inducing breathlessness, and then through the imposed silence of the poem's end. This silence, the 'breathless still place' that Graham invokes in 'The Nightfishing' (105–20), involves the recognition of the way that expiration and poetic conclusion are inextricably linked:

> So I spoke and died.
> So within the dead
> Of night and the dead
> Of all my life those
> Words died and awoke.

Death constitutes the awakening of words, but involves the disappearance or decay of the body that gives them voice. Breathing out in the process of speaking leads to expiration at the poem's end, an expiration that is somehow necessary in order for the words to come to life in the reader's affective response.

This response, for Graham, is deeply tied up with the representation and presentation of pain, the sensation which is placed beyond question. The pain at confronting absence is presented as both insistent and quotidian, almost mundane: it is unavoidable, and linked not to monumental historical events, but to the everyday actions of daily life such as washing 'the front of my face'. It can only be expressed by making present the figure of the departed addressee, whose presence is configured through situation within (and movement through) a particular geographical location.

Graham's elegiac memory depends not only on the specificity of location but also on the possibility of conceiving of presence within and movement through space. In 'Imagine a Forest' (pp.204–5), the imperative acts as an invocation of the reader who then becomes the subject of the poem's first two four-line sentences. The speaker says of the imagined forest:

> You are walking in it and it sighs
> Round you where you go in a deep
> Ballad on the border of a time
> You have seemed to walk in before.

This poem asks me, as reader, to imagine that I'm in a 'real' place, somewhere that seems familiar. It places me in a forest, controlling my (imagined) location. It is not until the poem's eleventh line that the speaker acknowledges this control over my location within the poem, naming the speaking 'I' as pronoun and subject: 'I have set you here and it is not a dream / I put you through'. By reading the poem I am put in a particular (if unspecified) position; I am made present by and within the poem, situated in a location that is both geographically 'real' and poetically imagined.

The 'you' of 'Lines on Roger Hilton's Watch' (235–37) works in a very different manner. As addressee, the watch acts as a form of representative (if not synecdoche) for its absent owner. It triggers some sort of associative memory, as the speaker contemplates the actions of the watch's 'master', again playing with the sounds of place-names with the 'Botallack tick'. However, the status of the object is altered somewhat by the change of speaker: this addressee is one who is given the opportunity to speak.

> He picks me up and holds me
> Near his lonely face
> To see my hands. He thinks
> He is not being watched.

Although it is 'only a watch', the poem recognises the word's semantic potential, suggesting that the 'I' who looks back might be some sort of vigil or even simply the act of looking, a suggestion supported by the timepiece's anthropomorphic 'hands'. Hilton's watch occupies a strange space between metaphor and metonymy. Through his implicit identification with his watch he is transferred into a different semantic realm, while the contiguity of the metonymy that depends on his ownership of and apparent existence within the watch transports him to the location of the poem's setting as he is able to observe the figure of the Graham-speaker.

Watkin claims that while elegy is a central part of metaphor's process of dissolving the body into spirit, metonymy approaches the gap by working through more physical and causal relationships.[8] In Graham's poetry it becomes clear that what Watkin terms the 'gap between figure and referential reality' is in fact much more complicated than he allows. Graham's poetry does not allow the possibility of either erasing or filling this gap, nor of jumping over it; the relationship between speaker and addressee is every bit as complicated as that between the pronoun or signifier 'you' and its potential referents, the person or persons to which it might refer.

Notes

[1] All references are to W.S. Graham, *New Collected Poems* (London: Faber, 2004). Page references are given after quotations in the text.
[2] Tony Lopez, *The Poetry of W.S. Graham* (Edinburgh: Edinburgh University Press, 1989), p.76.
[3] W. S. Graham, 'Notes on a Poetry of Release', in *The Nightfisherman: Selected Letters of W.S. Graham*, ed. by Michael Snow and Margaret Snow, (Manchester: Carcanet Press, 1999), pp. 379–83, p.382.
[4] Ibid., p.381.
[5] William Watkin, *On Mourning: Theories of Loss in Modern Literature* (Edinburgh: Edinburgh University Press, 2004), p.101.
[6] Ibid., p.169.
[7] W. S. Graham, *The Nightfisherman: Selected Letters of W.S. Graham*, ed. by Michael & Margaret Snow. (Manchester: Carcanet Press, 1999), p.162.
[8] Watkin, p.60.

Footwork

Jane Routh

There's a photograph of a pair of very worn old-fashioned walking boots inside Jonathan Williams's *Shankum Naggum*. Here and there across its pages are boot prints; inside the back cover those boots reappear covered in mud. That was 1979. I think Thomas A. Clark's still out there somewhere on his daily walks that generated the detached aphorisms of 'In Praise of Walking'—whose variety of mood and vista suggests years of footwork—but if you've got your walking boots on these days, I guess you're more likely to run into a visual artist than you are a poet. (Clark's unusual anyway, in taking walking as subject matter as well as process. For all the images, Williams's pamphlet isn't *about* boots.)

The territory of walking *as subject* is staked out by Hamish Fulton and Richard Long, and to lesser degrees by other 'environmental' artists. Tom Phillips dates the beginnings of such work like this: 'Many artists took to their heels in the early seventies, and much art, including some of my own included walking'.[1] Phillips's own walks were urban, and he soon developed his own 'mapwalks' to include periodicity and chance to generate more of the action. 'Peckham is not Peru however and it was harder than I thought to extrapolate symbols of any great eloquence from these mean streets'.

Richard Long's walks are often specified in some detail in the captions of the photographs which he uses to characterise and typify the experience, such as *A Line of 164 Stones. A Walk of 164 miles. A walk across Ireland, placing a nearby stone on the road at every mile along the way.* Hamish Fulton however has always insisted that the walk *itself* is the work—something which has proved problematic for gallery curators, since exhibition catalogues often tie themselves in knots about the work displayed on the walls. (And possibly its price labels.) Is this the art work, or something different? How does the one relate to the other? 'My artform is the short journey', Fulton says simply.[2] The artefacts which he produces afterwards for gallery walls or posters or books and which can be bought and sold are something different. They can't (and he never suggests that they can) transcribe the experience of the walk which is about an attempt at being 'broken down' mentally and physically—with the desire to 'flow' inside a rhythm of walking—to experience a temporary state of euphoria, a blending of my mind with the outside world of nature.[3]

•

New Year's Day. I set off to walk up Ingleborough. On the steep bit that slows you down a man who'd got up earlier than me was scrambling down fast: *oodloodle*, then: *hello mate, great, yeh, dunno, 's right, yeh maybe, great.* He sat on a rock and lost his pace. I lost my walk: the mountain could have been any high street, any train. At least he didn't start taking phone-pictures of the view to relay to the mate. A mobile phone as essential as Landranger map and a compass?

Father Hopkins would not have thought so. (Have you ever noticed how often he uses the word *trod*? He was a walker all right.) He wasn't at all keen on company: 'even with one companion ecstasy is almost banished: you want to be alone and feel that.' The trouble with company that bright day in the Alps he grumbled, was that 'the cold feet, the spectacles, the talk and the lunching came in.'[4] Ah, the talk. A walk in company brings the horizon down to the domestic and the lunch boxes. I'm surprised to find Thomas A. Clark so tolerant: 'In the course of a walk, we usually find out something about our companion, and this is true even when we travel alone.'[5] Or maybe he's politely glossing over what Father Hopkins bemoaned. No matter how carefully we choose our companion, solitary walks will take us deeper. Alone, you hear, you see a thousand things you would not in company, and that's not just because your loud talk about the best spot to have lunch forewarns every wild thing around you to step back into the shadows long before you're near.

The attention that would have been given to the companion's cold feet, spectacles and need for his lunch before you go too much further is given to the world. Talk gives way to a silence in which your own footfalls are quietened, no longer careless of twigs snapping underfoot. You are attuned not to human presence, but to what's beyond you. You see more, you hear more, yes, but you *sense* more too. After all, you too are animal.

·

I'm fortunate in living where the scattered small farms of the last few centuries have left a web of footpaths across the hills and valleys, farm to farm, to school, to church. And there's Open Access land nearby. Walking here doesn't have to be planned: you can be distracted by the day's low sun through the trees above the river and be off down the field without even thinking about it.

One of my broken resolutions a few years ago was to write notes about some of these rambles. Not as the basis for any other sort of writing, but so that I didn't forget how I was always encountering something remarkable. This from an entry one March:

> Between the two woodpiles there was a stag, a big fellow, very dark, a six-pointer with velvet on his antlers. He didn't hear my steps, perhaps for the river's perpetual chatter; he didn't smell my humanity perhaps for the wild garlic reeking its tender new shoots out of wet earth. He looked at me from time to time but I stood tree-still...[He]strolled closer and closer—the closest I have ever been to a deer. He wrenched such great gobfuls of new growth up from the beach no wonder nothing grows if not in deer-guards. Not a pretty face: short and fat, hamster-like. I was all in dark, but my pale face began to puzzle him: he looked me in the eye a long time and then thought just to be on the safe-side he'd bound upwards a little, but nonchalantly as if to show that he wasn't really bothered about a mere tree/person. Such relief to move *my* legs: and when I did, the whole woodland above me exploded in a scattering of hinds, their white targets shooting off in all directions.

This is not so extraordinary; this entry's one of many similar. Nor so out-of-the-way, either: the encounter took place (I've just looked at the map) 400 yards from a bus route. But in company, I wouldn't have been aware of the creature before it became aware of me. Now it isn't just the obvious—that one person makes less noise than two, so creatures have plenty of warning to secrete themselves—so much as that on your own, your eyes and ears are on the out-there. I often feel deer before I see them, because of how they run through the woods. It's not exactly a sense of earth shaking, not quite a sound below your normal range; the drumming of hooves on ground is something you feel in your body.

Yes, sitting still out in the countryside, you might also see a deer. This is not the point: walking is a particular way of being on the land. You attend to the ground underfoot; you attend to distance and relative nearness, space and direction, *as well as* all the fortuitous encounters with creatures and things along the way. 'Walking in the hills', says Hamish Fulton, 'allows the possibility of blending mind and body with the land.'[6] There's a natural pace and a rhythm that each place calls up, the slow stride on short turf, the short step up rough hillside. It's this walking pace that Gary Snyder recounts recognising when he was told a Dreamtime story by a Pintupi elder while driving across Australia's central desert. Stories were told so quickly, one crowding into another, that Snyder says 'I couldn't keep up. I realized after about half an hour of this that these were tales meant to be told while walking, and that I was experiencing a speeded-up version'.[7]

•

Walking's good for you. It can help prevent heart disease, keep weight down and 'improve your mental well-being', as you too will have read somewhere recently. I suppose the well-being bit is about dopamine release and that will do anybody good, poets included. Even Fulton says he's 'discovered that if I don't exercise, my chemistry goes cranky'.[8] But of more particular benefit may be his 'blending' with the land. You walk away from the chatter of everyday. You can't fail to attend to something beyond your own self. Simply and practically, you'll trip, you'll get lost / wet / dirty if you don't take account of the terrain. You're aware of something larger than yourself, larger than this self-referential world we've made for ourselves. Humankind and its stuff isn't everything. You can get yourself in perspective and stop expecting that the tightly turned-in world we've made for ourselves can satisfy all our needs; it can't. We've always been part of something bigger, always—until very recently in our lifetime—been confronted by something that humankind hasn't touched.

The Ramblers Association says that 77% of UK adults walk for pleasure at least once a month. I'm astonished. That's something like 40 million people but only 2 of them have walked on the footpath past my garden this month. Maybe that many like to *say* they walk that much. For the most we're cut off from the land. Our contemporary separation from the more-than-human-world is something which ecopsychologists name as the source of illnesses (both mankind's own, as well as the planet's.) This is one of the reasons why 'wilderness' has become the setting for many therapies and group ventures. 'Wilderness is a way and a tradition in its own right. If we are willing to be still and open enough to listen, wilderness itself will teach us' says Stephen Harpur, who runs wilderness workshops at Big Sur.[9] What these set out to achieve is an enlivening of the senses, an awareness of time and distance as something in which we can trust our own experience, and a reclamation of instinct and personal wildness. What's been projected on to the natural world— possibly as something feared—is taken back into ourselves. It follows that our own psyche is integrated in the web of nature and therefore that our own health depends on that of the planet.

Of course an OS map and a footpath are cheaper. It's not the therapy I'm concerned with anyway, but the process. It's away from day to day clatter and at our own pace and in our own rhythm that we'll get somewhere more profound. One thing the walk certainly does is get us back into our bodies, in the simplest and most ordinary way. Thank goodness. I think that's why I like the muddy boots photograph in *Shankum Naggum*.

To walk isn't necessarily to write about ecology any more than it is to write about walking itself. 'Walking is about an investment of time,' says Fulton, 'the time of your life'.[10] It is also a way of breaking our increasing intercourse solely with our own signs and fabrications. 'A world where everything speaks of us is both a noisy world and a lonely one—we're everywhere, and we're all there is.'[11] That's Bill McKibben. And within this noisy world, what happens according to David Abrams is that

Human awareness folds in on itself, and the senses— once the crucial site of our engagement with the wild and animate earth—become mere adjuncts of an isolate and abstract mind.[12]

I'd like to be able to argue simply that a solitary walk is one of the few occasions you can encounter the more-than-human world, whatever wild is left to us, as well as one of the few occasions you can encounter the more you also are, the wilder person. I'd like to be able to quote Thomas A. Clark and leave it at that:

> That something exists outside ourselves and our preoccupations, so near, so readily available, is our greatest blessing.[13]

But I can only go so far as to say that it's probably the closest we can come, the best we can do. If the fatty tissues of polar bears contain industrial compounds from a world away, wherever we are we shall always now be in some senses 'necessarily accompanied by the rest of the race'.[14]

Notes

[1.] Tom Phillips, *Works and Texts* (Thames and Hudson, London, 1992) p.136.
[2.] Quoted by Andrew Wilson in Hamish Fulton, *Walking Journey* (London: Tate Publishing, 2002) p.21.
[3.] Fulton, *ibid*, p.27.
[4.] Gerard Manley Hopkins, Journal entry for July 25th 1868.
[5.] Thomas A. Clark, 'In Praise of Walking', *Distance and Proximity* (Edinburgh: pocketbooks, 2000) p.17.
[6.] Hamish Fulton, *Wild Life* (Edinburgh, pocketbooks, 2000) p.191.
[7.] Gary Snyder, *The Practice of the Wild* (San Francisco: North Point Press, 1990) p.82.
[8.] *Walking Journey, op. cit.*, p.200.
[9.] 'The Way of Wilderness' in T. Roszak, M. Gomes & A. Kanner, *Ecopsychology* (San Francisco: Sierra Club Books, 1995) p.185.
[10.] *Walking Journey, op. cit.*, p.202.
[11] *ibid*, p.19.
[12.] David Abrams, *The Spell of the Sensuous* (New York: Pantheon, 1996) p.267.
[13.] *op. cit.* p.15.
[14.] *Walking Journey, op. cit.* p.19.

The Whole World's Water

Penelope Shuttle

> The whole world's water at some time or another
> Flows through the Carrick Roads......
>
> Peter Redgrove, from 'Living In Falmouth'

My husband the poet Peter Redgrove, died on Bloomsday, 16th June 2003, from a combination of Parkinson's Disease and diabetes. My father Jack Shuttle died six months later, on 7th December.

Like making love for the first time or giving birth to your first child, their dark negatives, the deaths of spouse or parent brings feelings you could never have predicted.

There's no way of preparing for such events.

Everything you've imagined, trying the situation on like a garment in a shop, is useless.

For just over a month in the midsummer of 2003 I sat, with our only child Zoe, at Peter's bedside, knowing his hospital bed was his death bed.

He was semi-conscious, as he had been on admission to the High Dependency Unit. Now he was in the Renal Unit, his kidneys failing. He'd been given dialysis, but his kidneys just wouldn't work.

On May 14th, he'd been taken to hospital by ambulance. Unable to get out of bed that morning, he'd been diagnosed with a possible spontaneously-fractured hip, for he also suffered severe arthritis. The paramedics gave him gas and air to get him downstairs. The two men used a sort of hoisting chair, the bigger of the burly twosome squatting on his hindquarters behind Peter, gripping him as they bumped down from stair to stair. 'Have a nice time', Peter murmured to me as he was lifted into the ambulance. These were the last coherent words he spoke.

When he reached the casualty department he became, in the doctor's jargon, *combative,* and very disoriented. We learned later that this was caused by the infection he'd contracted, maybe on a recent visit to London. He fought the doctor and nurses, was given an injection of diazepam, and never fully recovered consciousness, as the sepsis took hold.

They sent me home. Just as I was going to bed, the duty doctor rang to say they feared Peter was dying. His heartbeat was very rapid, he wasn't passing any urine, and they feared organ failure. By the time I got over there, he'd stabilized slightly. After a fortnight in the HD Unit he was moved to the Renal ward.

Every afternoon Zoe and I read poems to him, mostly his own, plus a few of his favourites, Wallace Stevens, Rilke... Sometimes he responded a little, at others he fretted and whimpered, trying to pull the drip from his throat, cowering away whenever a nurse approached, making inarticulate panicky sounds.

My stepson Bill Redgrove spent the mornings with Peter. By now the Renal Consultant had told us there was no hope of Peter recovering. They'd withdrawn the tube by which Peter was being fed and receiving every antibiotic under the sun, and upped the morphine dose. 'He'll have an easy death', said the doctor, 'No pain, and lovely dreams all the time.' In the middle of the morning on the 16th June, with Bill holding his hand, he died.

Bloomsday

You died on Bloomsday 03,
nearly midsummer,
the day back in 57
Plath married Hughes,
under the rushed electrification
of a cloud

The wild orchids are over,
just a dry lip-reading of stems
in the old flower meadow
unploughed since 1914

Memory's travelling circus
frees its lions and tigers,
they lope into a world without bars,
and friends take me to visit
the house where you and I first met,
far from town,
in the lee of serious hills

We can't go in,
strangers live there now,
but its enough to be in the lane,
under February clouds,
remembering our midsummer meeting,

how my books, my ear-rings
fascinated you,
and how I, chaste
as a line of poetry it takes a lifetime to write,
let down my defences, took an endless step towards you

★ ★ ★

What a day to choose,
considering Joyce
was not one of your heroes
(read, yes, respected, yes,
not loved) —
why not choose Yeatsday
or Jungsday? Langlandsday
or Wallace Stevensday?
But then you didn't choose it,
it chose you,
freeing you from your month-long deathbed,
your son, not mine,
holding, then relinquishing, your hand

★

For at least a year prior to Peter's death, I'd been very depressed, due to the combined strain of being his fulltime carer and the pain of witnessing his decline over a number of years from a man of exceptional vigour to an invalid. Despite his physical frailty he was, however, intellectually unimpaired. Tiring easily, he nevertheless spent two or three hours a day at his typewriter, working on poems, right up until the day before he was admitted to hospital.

After his death, my depression intensified to inchoate misery. How can this be? I asked myself, and everyone. How can Peter not be here? How can I endure this?

I felt overwhelmed by time, didn't know how to get through it. Every hour lasted three hours, every day went on for a week. I wanted to sleep all the time, staying in bed or dozing on the sofa, sometimes taking a sleeping pill in the daytime. Zoe moved back to Cornwall after Peter died, and she was my lifeline. But poetry vanished from my life. I stopped going to my yoga class, my poetry workshop and my meditation group. The cowed spirit in me wanted oblivion, sleep.

Grief makes the world black and white, like an old-fashioned newsreel. Even the rainbow or the peacock's tail turns black and white. Sunset loses its colours. Even my dreams lacked colours. I didn't want to go out of the house. All the walks were part of Peter and me; their colour and purpose had vanished. How could I walk down to the sea now, or to the public gardens, where, in all weathers, we read out poems from our favourite anthologies?

What was the point? And I wept all the time.

Weeping

I wept in Tesco,
Sainsburys
and in Boots

where they gave me
medicine for grief

But I wept in Asda,
in Woolworths
and in the library

where they gave me
books on grief

I wept in Clarks,
looking in vain for shoes
that would stop me weeping

I wept on the peace march
and all through the war

I wept in Superdrug
where they gave me
a free box of tissues

I wept in the churches,
the empty empty churches,

and in the House of Commons —
they voted me out of office

*

From June 03 until the following spring I inhabited this colourless world. Then two turning points brought colour and an initial measure of acceptance into my life.

During this very raw time, our good friend Eleanor took me out for drives. One afternoon in that first spring without Peter we went to an old house near Penryn called Enys. No-one lives there any more, the house is shut-up, but a Trust keeps the garden going and sometimes the grounds are open to the public. We went there to see the bluebells for which Enys is justly famed. It was a sunny windy April afternoon. The bluebells don't just grow in glades and under trees but spread out in vast open acres. I walked round the perimeter of the bluebell field.

In the warm sun a wonderful perfume drifted up from the bluebells. The flowers, the warmth and the reality of spring, the many other visitors visibly enjoying the gardens—all this unlocked the fetters of loss. Colours began to return. I still felt grief like a violent hand at my throat, but time was no longer made up of endless hours, began offering possibilities.

Peter and I had often come to Enys in the spring. This visit brought the past back, not in anguish, as had been the case for months, but in consolation, a gift from the earth.

This is what Peter wrote about the bluebells at Enys.

Reservoirs of Perfected Ghost

> Acres of the sky having
>> floated down and settled in the woods,
>>> the bluebell canopy spreads beneath
> The green capes of the trees;
>> heaven is so full of sky
>>> it cannot hold it—it falls
> Into the woods, and spreads, heaven
>> skygazing in its woodland cavern;
>>> bend down and pluck with admiration
> A juicy stem; the blue bell
>> salivates glass-juice on your fingers;
>>> lift this flower to your nose
> It smells not at all!
>> it is all of them that smells:
>>> the sun reaches through the leaves
> And lifts the perfume out, gently
>> from these masses, so as not to break it; keeping
>>> the shock of the blueness
> As it issues from underground;
>> heaven must have gone deep,
>>> to arrive so.

*

After Peter's funeral, Zoe stripped his bed, tidied his room up, and shut the door. I didn't go back in there for months. But my second turning point was a sudden and spontaneous decision to go into Peter's room, shortly after that visit to the bluebells. On his desk I found a thick file of his last poems. The first poem I read was 'The Harper', full of Peter's characteristic delight in water, evoking vividly so much of Peter's personality, his fascination with all life, in this instance a water beetle, and the exactitude with which he explored water, nature, but always putting the human experience in balance within it. Here are a few lines from 'The Harper':

> Shiny waterbeetles
> scribe the pond, each one
>   the centre of its circular signature,
>
> Each one the centre
> of its circular harp ...

Reading Peter's last poems brought poetry back into my life. After a long silence, I relished reading and writing it. Like the beetles scribing the pond I took up my role as scribe.

The visit to Enys and the crossing of the threshold into Peter's room freed me from much grief; I know it will always be there, but the terrible inertia of the double-bereavement abated, and I began to write about grief. The act of articulating grief enabled me to find a way of living with my sadness.

Without a kiss from a prince, my spirit woke from grief's slumber-spell.

Now I began walking again, rejoining friends at the Falmouth Footpath Society; our forays along the coast and into the heart of Cornwall continued the process of healing.

Often when I'm walking, in company, or alone, I think of those favourite writers of mine for whom walking was so important; John Cowper Powys, Virginia Woolf, Edward Thomas, following in their footsteps in both senses, as walker, as reader.

Peter liked to say that when you're walking you're going at God's Speed. God travels on foot, he insisted, at about three miles an hour. How I missed our long walks, all over The Lizard, and along the north coast of Cornwall; Peter's health deteriorated and he could only manage a painful walk to the beach five minutes away from home. In a way, I began grieving for Peter a year or more before his death, as our life experiences narrowed, and we were constantly challenged to find value in our life when so much was being stripped away from us. We were living in the middle of an elegy.

Walking brings you in an equal relation to nature. For me, the act of walking is to experience the poetry of the body; breath, muscles, joints, all co-operating, like stresses in a line, lines in a stanza.

This year I've been on walking holidays in Devon with the walking club, in Andalucia with Zoe, and on my own in Boscastle. Every step on every walk was one more step away from that first year of desolation.

My first sustained piece of writing after Peter's death was a sequence of twenty poems called *Missing You*. Here I try to convey the sense of separating myself from Peter.

Letting Go of You

I'm letting go of you
year by year
Today it was 1970,
tomorrow it may be 1977

There is so much of you,
you will never completely cease,

but slowly
I'm releasing some of you from me,

there's no rush, no deadline,
time doesn't matter,

its just that I can't despair forever

so I pour you away from me,
libation by libation,

as if discarding the water
from the font at Manaccan
in which an infant has just been baptized

*

Poetry is the channel through which I let go of Peter and yet paradoxically stay in touch with him. Ours was a marriage of poets, poetry the touchstone of our life together. Via poetry I'm telling Peter things:

Telling You Things

You've gone,
but I tell you things all the time,

how lots of your ex-students came to your funeral,
what film I saw last night,

(*Silver City*—it was crap),

I tell you about the new ferry to Trelisssick,
the floods at Boscastle

You don't answer
but never mind—this one-sided conversazione
has its own magic,

like telling secrets to the bees, for good luck

Our daughter went out for a walk this evening—
'and everyone I passed was German'

Yes, it's holiday season again
Last year I slept through it,

afraid to leave the house
all that beautiful terrible summer,

not talking to you, or anyone
Now I tell you everything,

the way the lake looked
as autumn took charge of Italy,
how I flew over the Alps
in the meekest of planes,

I can't bear you to miss anything;
Life goes on. I keep bringing it to you,

the inexhaustible newness of time.

*

I've often drawn on my dreams for the raw material of poetry. Poetry and dreaming are both deep wells of imagination, using language in orthodox and unorthodox ways to reveal what Yeats called our 'secret working mind'.

For a long time after Peter died I didn't dream of him at all, until January 05 when I had this dream:

Peter and I are looking over a big appealing house with polished wooden floors. We go into a room with two hearths, one at either end, but no fires lit. We're planning to buy this house from a friendly old Scots couple, but only the wife is present, the man is away somewhere.

And from the dream came this poem:

Buying A House

This is the first time I've dreamed of you
since you died,
and we're buying a house,

the kind of house we always wanted,
enough room for all our books,
the cherished objects time swept into our laps,

like this fossil ammonite
with its brown hairline path travelling
to a centre and back out again,

undulating,
as if seen under water,
and this block of Icelandic spar

through which the seen world becomes the arctic;

the house has wooden floors,
the living room two hearths,
one at either end, both unlit

In the dream,
this lack of fire doesn't bother us,
though now I wonder why,

regretting the room
wasn't warmed by two blazing hearths,
one west, one east,

like those in the bar of The Tinners Arms
And the shadowy woman
showing us over the house,
where was her husband?

Was he out gathering firewood,
or was she a widow,
like me,

selling up, moving on?

There's another kind of walking I like, or rather walking/looking: visiting art galleries where one strolls slowly around but all the time being aware of the intense emotional core of the promenading. What are the pictures doing at a deep level, as one walks and pauses, walks and pauses?

The slow rhythmic pace of walking and looking often throws me into a light creative trance, in which the magic of paintings can flourish.

Whenever I'm in Tate Modern I go first of all to see Henri Matisse's *The Inattentive Reader*, his portrait of a girl with a book, not reading, but day-dreaming.

I've often written first drafts of poems standing in front of paintings and I wrote the following poem in such a way. It led me back to grief, but also opened a door on to the future.

The Inattentive Reader
Henri Matisse

I too am an inattentive reader,
lean my head on my hand,
like this girl who isn't reading her book

I also wait for answers
to my unpopular questions,
let time stand still behind me

Here are the girl's flowers,
her mirror, carpet,
and here is my room,

not so very different

Like her, I have things on my mind,
turn to the future as to a stranger,
to the past as to a friend

She's conducting a masterclass in reverie,
with her talent for not-reading,
never losing the thread of her day-dream

If I could, Peter,
my ever-attentive reader,
I'd paint your portrait

over an old Flight into Egypt,
build you a house out of Mondays and Thursdays,
a boat from Fridays and Wednesdays
But no house, portrait or boat
tempts you back to life,
and as a painter is never truly confused about colours

so you are clear in your mind about your death;
the slightest fever heals you,
the simplest rain lets you fall

★ ★ ★

In August 04 I was very sad to see the tv news pictures of a flooded
Boscastle. I was still flooded with grief myself and associated myself
very closely with Boscastle as in this poem.

Boscastle

I am Boscastle,
shocked as a shipwrecked sailor.
My two rivers,
The Jordan and the Valency,
two water-genies
bursting out of their earthen bottles,
sweeps the car-park clean of cars,
shoving them out to sea.
Floodwaters beat me
with branches ripped from valley trees,

waterfalls jet from my windows and attics,
I scramble on to a roof – Rescue me! rescue me!
In all my hotels,
cataracts rush through doors,
spiriting furniture away on their crazy backs,
my bridges shatter, my witchcraft museum
undergoes ordeal by water,
instead of witch burning. My cats
hide in cupboards, not all my dogs
reach higher ground. At my parish boundary
my farmers climb on the roofs of their land-rovers.
The merchandise in my shops sinks below the waters,
my foundations shake.
I'm seen on the t v news as far away
as Portugal and Delhi. My lovers
all round the world weep as they see
what has befallen me.

*

Peter and I visited Boscastle on walking holidays almost every year
from 1972 until 2001. This summer ('05) I felt strong enough to make
a Boscastle pilgrimage. I also wanted to see how the village was coping
with the aftermath of that flood and to add my fourpennorth to the
revival of its tourism business.

Needless to say, I was aware of following in the jumbo-size footsteps of
Thomas Hardy, who returned to Boscastle four months after the death
of his first wife Emma and where he wrote his great poems of grief.
In fact, I stayed in the Wellington Hotel in Boscastle, next door to the
Thomas Hardy room, where the poet had stayed.

During my four days at Bocastle, I walked and walked in wonderful high
summer weather, from Tintagel to Boscastle, inland to St Juliot and
Minster churches, and along the coast by Beeny and Pentargan cliffs.

No sooner had I got on the little bus at Truro and set off for the north
coast, poems cried out to be written. On every walk, I had to pause

constantly to get poems down in my notebook. I kept away from the crowds as much as possible and even in August I was able to find a secluded spot by the Valency, under some beech trees, to do my Chi Kung exercises of 'lifting the earth' and 'carrying the moon'.

Back in Falmouth, there are many unhappy memories of Peter's last years, and his struggle with Parkinson's etc, but in Boscastle I found only good memories of him, strong memories. I felt his presence everywhere, a powerful spirit free of life's burdens and pain but still interested in this world, and in me. All the time I was in Boscastle, it seemed I might see Peter at any moment, a sensation I have never felt at home since his death. Boscastle called his spirit ...

That sensation is beautifully conveyed in these lines from a poem about widowhood by Julia Casterton.

from The Rose Takes Over

You are the wife who has lost her husband,
the wife who does not mourn, but knows,
here among his poems and his deep thrown bowls

that you both always lived somewhere else,
really, and he has left you for that place.
His departure allows you to go there sometimes

in your earthly life, as now, you rinse dishes
by the kitchen window, gazing at a rose outside
that is always blown and always coming.

I feel that this poet has looked right into my heart and described how I feel after two years of widowhood, as if Boscastle is that 'somewhere else' which was a spiritual home for Peter and me.

Here's one of the dozen poems I wrote on my walks around Boscastle. The gatehouse chapel of Our Lady of Fontevrault is down the hill from the main church in Tintagel, St Materiana.

Gatehouse Chapel:
Our Lady of Fontevrault, Boscastle

No bigger than my garage,
this age-old rough-walled chapel,
is dark despite bright August outside,
just two small slim candles,
one I've lit for Peter, one for Dad;
silent sanctuary of Our Lady of Fontevrault,
Lady revered by Eleanor of Aquitaine—
silent abode of the spirit —

I come here with no Christian heart,
but in need of silence
offering itself to any faithless pilgrim —

On the granite window ledge
the book is open at the Psalms —
I am poured out like water ...
and my heart is like wax ...'

This isn't my first visit —
we came here years ago —
and silence set its crowns
of blessing on our heads,
like a Russian wedding

Now I've been bent
on the bow of sorrow,
the arrow of tears
shot into my own eye

As David put his trust in the Lord,
I put mine in the silence
ripening in this stone vineyard,

a quiet that sings
only where earth and time meet

This year
I've had my fair share of mosques and cathedrals
but nowhere found a silence
to suit me till I came here—
and though I was never an ill-treated wife,
in this chapel
dedicated to such women

I can weep,
like Eleanor, mother-in-law
of Berengaria daughter of King Sancho
the Wise ...
When I get home
I check my diary, yes, I hadn't wept
since March 14th 2004,

it was the right time and place
for weeping,
no longer the wild weeping of my first grief,
but brief simple tears
bequeathed to me by silence ...

*

One hot September day, I took the coast path from Falmouth to
Maenporth Beach three miles away. It was, give or take a day or two,
the first anniversary of the scattering of Peter's ashes into the sea off
Maenporth, a place he loved and often wrote about.

Nine friends came with us, waiting at the top of the beach while Zoe
and I carried Peter's ashes down to the water's edge. The tide was a long
long way out. Sunlight glittered on the wet ridges of sand and in the little
rivulets left behind by the tide. Mr. Lukey the undertaker had brought
Peter's ashes the previous day. It had been fifteen months before I was
able to deal with the ashes ... To my surprise, as Mr Lukey undid the red

velvet drawstring bag, they were not in an urn, but in a large sturdy red plastic tub, the exact shape and size of those old-fashioned glass sweetie jars you used to see in shops.

Zoe and I waded out into the waves. I unscrewed the lid and tipped the grey gritty ash into the sunlit water. The clear sea swirled them away with incredible rapidity. There was a sudden cloudiness in the water, and then his ashes were rushing away on the outgoing tide, as if Peter's mortal remains couldn't wait to become part of the sea, of the whole world's waters; as if he wanted to be part of the continuum of nature, and I'd kept him waiting too long (fifteen months! I hear him say). And the sea, it seemed, couldn't wait to welcome him.

Both Zoe and I had a sense of amazed release, of sheer surprise at the speed of Peter's transit. Bob, a friend, came across the beach to meet us, carrying three passion flowers which his wife Mary had sent, and we set these down on the beach. Then I read aloud Peter's poem 'The Idea of Entropy at Maenporth Beach' and we went up to Dorothy's house nearby, to drink a glass of wine to Peter.

And my father? We're interring his ashes next month in a country churchyard in Surrey. I couldn't let Dad go without a poem. I read many anthologies featuring poems for funerals and chose this very simple poem by Alan Curtis to be carved on Dad's headstone.

Rest

The memories and love I leave behind
Are yours to keep
I have found my rest; I have turned my face
To the sun, and now I sleep.

*

Sometimes I have reiki, an ancient practice, a kind of laying-on of hands, a light pressure being applied to key sites on the body. The practitioner is a lady who has the sight. After one session, which I experienced as a profound meditative state, she told me she saw an elderly man standing in the door, dressed very well, quite a dandy.

He said, *don't worry, I'm free now, I can go wherever I like.* My father was such a snappy dresser. If Julie saw his spirit and heard those words, I interpret them as meaning Dad is free now from the traumatic memories of his wartime past. He had been a prisoner of the Japanese from the Fall of Singapore in 1942 to the end of the war in the Far East in August 1945, working as a slave labourer on the Death Railway; I hope his spirit is free. I've written most of this essay sitting at Dad's old desk. Let both Peter and Dad be free to go wherever they like, stepping barefoot into reality whenever they please.

2 October 2005
Falmouth, Cornwall

Notes on the poems

'Living in Falmouth' from Peter Redgrove, *From The Virgil Caverns* (Cape, 2001), copyright © Peter Redgrove, 2001. 'Reservoirs of Perfected Ghosts' and 'The Harper' from Peter Redgrove, *The Harper* (Cape, 2006), copyright © the Estate of Peter Redgrove, 2006. Reproduced here by permission of Penelope Shuttle.

'Weeping', 'Letting Go of You' and 'The Inattentive Reader' from Penelope Shuttle, *Redgrove's Wife* (Bloodaxe Books, 2006), copyright © Penelope Shuttle, 2006. Reproduced here by permission of Penelope Shuttle.

'Bloomsday', 'Telling You Things', Buying A House', 'Boscastle' and 'Gatehouse Chapel: Our Lady of Fontevrault, Boscastle' are published here for the first time and are copyright © Penelope Shuttle, 2007.

'The Rose Takes Over' from Julia Casterton, *The Doves of Finisterre* (The Rialto, 2004), copyright © Julia Casterton, 2004. Reproduced here by permission of The Rialto.

'Rest' by Alan Curtis, copyright © 2004, Alan Curtis, reproduced here by permission of Jonathan Clowes Ltd, on behalf of Julia Watson.

Walking, Interference

Lawrence Upton

I walk a lot; and I walk most in West Penwith, the westernmost extremity of Cornwall. It is almost an island and can be walked across in a long day. It's being down-sized by the urban; and undermined by sea-rise. The roads are nonsensical. Everything is in the same direction, or opposite-pointing roads go eventually to the same place.

Green roads developed; then, their purpose ended, decayed. Dead ends may be explicated with attention: a quarry or a mill or a mine or a farm abandoned. Time folds and stretches and doubles back as one walks between the ruins of 6000 years. Those granite places are part of me even if I don't know what they are. How could I? I don't know what I am. I don't know what Cornwall is. I stand on it much as an insect stands on a leaf.

It is a low wage economy with no legacy of affluence. Those silent ivy-covered ruins so many take as signs of 'romantic Cornwall' have the silence of absence and stagnation. Cornish economic migration generally has been as high at least as any country in Europe. When the rest of Britain prospers, Cornwall gets a few closeable shop branches and regional depots; and the profit daily crosses the Tamar eastwards.

West Penwith is not much written about unsentimentally, with the exception of D M Thomas. I walk there; I write poetry—for me, actions uneasily separated.

I have a memory fulcrum at Botallack. When I sought the solar eclipse of 1999, the nearest I've been to a church attendance in 40 years, it was far down the cliffs at the Crown Mine engine house. I wrote poems on my *search* for the eclipse; none about the event. I could describe it in terms of what I saw and felt which included crying. I could attempt explanation of what I saw, why I felt cold when I did etc. I have no idea why I cried; but I was crying at home. Of that, I have nothing to say. There *is* nothing to say. The eclipse is describable, the experience beyond my words. Normally I have so many words, like the streams of the small moors.

My response, after recovery of equilibrium, was animal. I wanted to do it again and researched how I could be in another total eclipse. It was a little like being chained to an idiot, in the words attributed to Aristotle on sexual desire.

It would not have been enough to have been in Cornwall, even to have been somewhere in West Penwith—like my friend, Alaric Sumner, on the Clodgy at St Ives, facing the other way because there were more data that way and therefore more to learn. I wanted perhaps to be as near as possible to the occluded sun; and knocked 10 miles off the 93 million; then climbed down into some danger to ensure I was alone. And *that* brought me round in one circle of my life though the details are uninteresting—I had thought it would have words, but it was a non-verbal yearning.

Walking is an engagement with the world. One goes where one wants, barbed wire permitting, and that is consuming. It may make the beginnings of poetry, words outside the conversational polity, potentially of it. It invigorates memories. Not so much what one might have said as what one wishes had not been said.

Hurtful things are bad enough. Untrue things are worse. It is better to be silent ...

Only in the making of poetry is there any chance of not, finally, expressing falsehood. And somehow this is a good landscape for it. I mean, not falsehood which can be wheedled around, but the speech vandalism which avoids commitment when it is due, expanding self till it is a weight.

Sumner explored an aspect of this in his play for voices *Conversation in colour*. Two lovers are shocked and inhibited by the illness of one, which confines him, and by desire to declare love. The play ends when, narratively and syntactically, there is no alternative, without violation of their wills, to the unqualified declaration: I love you.

It is a set of evasions, and anxieties resulting from evasion which move to and from necessity. One is static, the other is walking, at varying speeds, sometimes rushing, to and from the one who is static but otherwise vocal. Both are infected by regret full of hope and by hope full of regret, knowledge of the past, nostalgia for it, awareness of the present. The tone is inevitably elegiac whenever the loss inherent in their narrative is accepted; and the more the loss is accepted, the more it is ameliorated by them, for the present. There is no future. Only past, and present. But *that* cannot be avoided by denial. They are not that free. What is free? Their expression is patterned, repetitive and varying. There is no stage set. They are made of and imprisoned by their own words, and delineated by the pathos of their verbal situation.

There is no word that might be with a god here, no sense of a fresh naming. Their language is clichéd *because they are not being ventriloquised by an inspiration from outside themselves*. It is achieved by complex authorial patterning! The words they use have been someone else's words, as if bricks from ruins were being repatterned: the same thing and something different. The originality of the speeches is in syntactical ingenuity and syntactical echoing; otherwise we have quite literally heard it all before, as one nearly always has in habitual intimacy. They speak freely and they are constrained, as the text itself is structurally constrained.

Poetry *means* in a different way to summarisable texts. John Arlott remarked that 'if poetry means anything it means what it means to its readers', which gives a great deal of power to the reader and allows for a constant renewal in meaning without compromise. Sumner would have agreed whole-heartedly with Arlott, though he got to that position by an entirely different route.

Philip Payton wrote: 'In the fabric of the landscape, geology is in Cornwall [...] a powerful determinant of territorial character and identity.' Yet, in the writing of Sumner, with one notable exception, there is little recognition of landscape and none of the history it created. It affects neither his content nor his form. Sumner might have been writing anywhere. He was a knowledgeable bird-watcher, an accurate observer. He loved walking, especially the cliff path. Yet, apart from 'Waves on Porthmeor Beach', he seems not to have integrated those concerns with his writing. Landscape intrudes, typically seen out of a moving window. Birds have a section to themselves in 'Rhythm to intending'; but that really predates his long term presence outside London; and in it he speaks of things he has seen here and there rather than events within a specific landscape through which he moves.

There's quite a bit of West Cornwall in 'Text Out Of Image (Sandra Blow)', St Ives out of season, for instance; but the poet is reading paintings made in the landscape, not the landscape itself. I cannot think of a single poem or even section of Sumner's writing where he responds directly to an event or an object specifically in West Cornwall or South Devon.

A great deal of 'Waves on Porthmeor Beach' is direct observation, but of a small range of events; and there is also considerable later addition and reframing.

Over much of a year, Sumner went out and looked at the waves on the beach and wrote down what he saw, recording date, time and position. When he was away, he noted that. He was at pains to vary the time of day, and the position, of his observations. He serviced a process. The personal response, therefore, is, rendered indirectly; and then he reworked it to focus upon the act of writing. And once that writing was done, he did not return to such material and process.

Over his life, he took an enormous number of snap-photographs of the built and the shaped environment; yet showed no interest in the history of environments. His imagination responded to what was happening in its now or very recent past. While I was shocked by his uninterest, he was not dismayed by my enthusiasm. He accepted it and even listened to me if I insisted on telling him when something was built and by whom, a kindly passive challenge to my assumption to match his more positive and overt challenges to other more dangerous prejudices.

With 'Waves on Porthmeor Beach', Sumner has *changed* my way of looking, not by the shallower means of creating associations, but by deepening my understanding of the phenomenon and the intellectual mechanics of its perception, and how one might depict it. For me, he has created a phenomenology of Porthmeor Beach which is quite transportable; and my life is the richer.

Sumner collected linguistic detritus, which he took back to his desk to use. Words did not come readily to him by the act of writing. Though there is much original writing in his notebooks, there are even more possible starting points where a formal mechanism has occurred to him.

He enjoyed walking, but it was separated from the writing. Sumner had no time for the idea that one might come into fruitful contact with Wordsworth's 'best objects': his reality was dialogical. His aesthetic might best be known by what can be grasped of his response to artists working in other media who respond strongly to landscape.

Sandra Blow is an obvious example because of their warm friendship and collaboration. There is also his colleague at Dartington College of Arts, John Drever, the electro-acoustic musician whom Sumner invited to collaborate with him.

Less well-known is his interest in the painting of Neil Canning, an artist with a long-standing association with Penwith. Sumner made contact with him; and out of that came a plan for collaboration.

And there is also Sumner's interest in the art of Stephen Lawson, previously undocumented, which he knew from Lawson's 'Forms of Light' exhibition of photography and sculpture at Talbot Rice, Edinburgh in 1988, if not before. Sumner possessed the exhibition catalogue and probably attended in person. He also made contact with the artist with a view to buying prints of his photographic work.

For Lawson, the idea comes first, it seems: 'Once I have found the place I must think how least to alter the idea to fit the place.' He builds his images from sequences of photographs taken to a schedule. There are hints there perhaps of Sumner's method in 'Waves on Porthmeor Beach', though Sumner's schedule was ad hoc. Sumner's emphasis was more on the *transformation* of the perceived external than on the perceived external itself.

Where I will turn off the radio and try to get myself into external silence, Alaric might turn it on or sit in a cafe. He describes himself and is described as a man sitting in cafes and writing. If someone spoke, it might well be included; as what he was reading might turn up years later, perhaps rewritten. In 'Waves on Porthmeor Beach' he notes when he was interrupted transcribing field-notes in public places. Interference of all kinds intrigued him greatly; and his essay 'Voices (for 9): postmodern performance?' speaks of some kinds of interference and aural overload as being *the* device underlying 'Voices (for 9)'.

When young, he wrote single poems; and never quite abandoned that. There is, for instance, a birthday poem for the artist Rory McDermott from the late 1990s. But increasingly he concentrated on sequences and larger pieces based. He wrote for theatre and for mixed- and inter-media events. His characters are not stable in terms of conventional notions of personality.

It is a writing of ideas. 'Conversation in colour' is apparently an impressive exception to that, but even there, the writing process is mediated through strong structural devices, both thematic and syntactical. Its resolution is ambiguous. Similar observations might be made of 'Voices (for 9)'. The writing largely operates within the world it invokes. In 'Tonight', that world and its language seem about to become one thing in some ways.

And there is a late poem, 'Survival', which muses on the fragility of a human body as a container of ideas and wishes for a 'less fragile container ...' which turns out to be electronic!

It is one of the few signs in his writing of an almost voracious appetite for SF. And, although it is avowedly materialist, as he always was, it also reminds me of more than one reader's remark since 'LETTERS for dear AUGUSTINE' was published, regarding a previously undemonstrated mysticism.

Any self-reflective process such as writing, especially writing over a period of time of something that is elusive, is likely to raise a ghost in its machine as modes of meaning generation clash. Knuth remarks that Science is what you can explain to a computer and the rest is Art; and in both orderings, Science and Art, with or without a computer, the question of purpose and meaning arises. Alaric, with his fervent adoption of Fish's 'Reader Response Theory', may sometimes have wondered where the predicate of his activity resided. If not outside in the world, then where inside? In the language? That still leaves us one fraction of a second after the Big Bang ...

I take *walking* to mean a great many things other than perambulation. My voluntary sometimes almost compulsive walks exist in tension with the concomitant writing down, involving physical stasis. Sometimes I get only a few hundred yards before I must find my notebook.

I try not to go out to write. There is a presumptive quality to that which disturbs my superstition. I think of it sideways, the writing, playing coaxing tricks on the inner dialogue which other circumstances delineate as conscience. By habitual observation and concentration, one is familiar with the behaviour of what one seeks; it is possible sometimes to reach out and take hold or be taken hold of.

Animals have us sussed. They know our eyes are our eyes, probably better than we do (one suspects they have fewer abstractions cluttering them) and that our mouths are our mouths; and so on. They know our behavioural patterns. They are off before we have commenced the lunge.

The mice who set up home in my Surrey study, while I was in Cornwall, learned, on my return, how my hands moved over the keyboard. In their curiosity I have had them sitting on the keyboard while I was typing before I caught and exiled them.

This informal mutual respect involves becoming aware of one's behaviour and learning to disjoint its syntax, so that the capturing / greeting gesture is in one movement with no preamble or other cue, not the last of a sequence of gestural rituals.

It makes for stillness and I am trying to learn that better if only to see what comes to sit beside me. Frequently I don't know what the creatures are; that is not the point. If I could classify them, I still wouldn't know their own names. And that is what I would like to know. I am grateful for their chatterless company.

A poem comes when any number of internal states are in tune but at rest with respect to each other. And that is likely when interference from the brain is at its lowest.

There are many kinds of interference. We howl, like analog radios, discords within and about our selves, jangling; and one must move one's thoughts in non-Euclidean directions to be rid of it.

The brain quietens when we are physically active too. I don't think the world seems any less bleak for a long walk; but I am generally less bothered by bleakness. As a firm shake of a frying pan or of a wheelbarrow will restore their contents to the kind of order we recognise, so a fast walk is likely to shake me into shape and even to induce a poem to flow.

It isn't anything entering the body like external breath, though it may seem like it. A sudden movement will cause the mammal moving between your feet to scurry, as it crosses before the gate you are leaning on; a proprietorial approach to an arriving poem will disrupt its receipt, like a horse shying at a premature swing of the horse box door.

Don't compel the poem. Don't look for it overtly. Be patient.

Reading forces one into sitting or lying down and I cannot conceive of making poetry without reading it. Too much reading and too little reading are disorders for this poet; while some not-walking is essential. When anything is being endured, it is too much.

Not walking includes use of trains and buses. Much of my writing is done on transport in notebooks and latterly a palm computer I've been given. Much is lost, much gained. I went from Paddington to Plymouth in the autumn of 2004, unable to write on anything, because of leaking headphones across the carriage which affected *my* ear adversely; but by the time I came to write down what was in my head, as we crossed now darkened Cornwall, the writing came out more dense and more orderly than it might have been.

I spend much of my year on the outskirts of a huge city and chunks on the edge of the Atlantic Ocean, an engine of power, which I watch from my window, able to lift and move the heaviest structures. It takes the unwary. I write in modest offices, but electronically equipped.

Thus, walking as / and inhabiting and / as reimagining are central to me as I come to know a landscape and its history more thoroughly than most of its inhabitants; and differently I expect, more abstractly, than my direct ancestors knew their own landscapes not far from here; and yet am not of it in other ways, finding myself somewhat outside my chosen community, seeking to live *in* the country while those around me seem to live on it.

Alaric Sumner: Life & Work

Alaric Sumner (1952–2000) was a poet, playwright, performance writer and visual artist. He was a member of Bob Cobbing's workshop in the mid-1970s and the founder of *words worth* magazine and Zimmer Zimmer Press. He became the first Writer-in-Residence at Tate St Ives and a part-time lecturer in Performance Writing at Dartington College of Arts. His poem for performance 'The Unspeakable Rooms' realised as a performance by Rory McDermott took both to North America. *Nekyia*, an opera for video, audio and live voice made with the composer Joseph Hyde was highly successful and is still presented as a film, a two-hander with Hyde and the singer Steve Halfyard and sometimes a three-hander with Lawrence Upton taking Sumner's part. There were many other collaborations with, among others, John Levack Drever and, separately, Lawrence Upton. His last public appearance was on 1 March 2000, launching his new poem 'Bucking Curtains' with a performance by him and Lawrence Upton

He died unexpectedly of an undiagnosed heart condition on 24 March 2000 at his home in St Ives, with the bulk of his writing still unpublished. In the autumn of 2004, the 'First Alaric Sumner Festival' was held over three days at Camden People's Theatre, supported by a number of organisations, including Dartington College of Arts and Contemporary Poetics Research Centre, Birkbeck College, and private donation. A foyer exhibition of his graphical works was extended to October and then until December.

Publications in print

(All published by and available from Writers' Forum unless otherwise indicated)

The flowering of atomic romanticism in the desolation of poetry, (1980?; reissued April 2005). Double-sided A4 sheet.

Aberrations of Lenses Mirrors Sight, (1998 / 2004) A4 comb-bound; 25pp.

Sumner's Nekyia Texts, (2005) 20 pp, A5 portrait.

Bucking Curtains, The Mainstream Poetry, (2000 / 2006) 16pp, A3 landscape.

VOICES (for 9) (2005); A3; 37 pp; comb-bound.

The Unspeakable Rooms (2003) A4; 16pp; comb bound. A4; 16pp; comb-bound.

The Unspeakable Rooms: a prescript of performance possibilities with Rory McDermott; (2004) A5 portrait; 8 pp.

Text out of image: Sandra Blow (2004) A4 portrait; 28pp

error studies and Portraits (2004) A4 portrait; 24 pp; some copies comb-bound.

Conversation in colour (2004) A4 portrait; 24pp; edited by Lawrence Upton.

LETTERS for dear AUGUSTINE—the semantic text i.e. excluding the graphic elements (2004) A4; 41pp; edited by Lawrence Upton; some copies comb-bound.

Voices (for 9): post-modern performance (2004) Writers Forum in association with *Realm of Stucco* and *words worth books*. A5 portrait; 16pp.

A Dutch Horizon published by *words worth books*; ISBN 0 906024 23 (words worth books) February 2005.

Domestic Ambient Buoys in discussion with Alaric Sumner August 1999, London (2005) A4 trimmed.

Coherent Language (2005) 32 pp A5 portrait.

The politics of performing art (2005) 19 pp A5 portrait.

Shock of the shock: extremeness in writing and performance, (2005) Cover is "title withheld" by Lawrence Upton; 32 pp A5 portrait; *Writers Forum*; December 2005; ISBN 1 84254 602 3

Portraits (2006)

Publications about Alaric Sumner

Remembering Alaric Sumner, a feature by Lawrence Upton published in
  Masthead 8—see also Alison Croggon's editorial. (See 'Further sources
  of information' below) Also available as *Remembering Alaric Sumner*
  from Writers Forum, A5 portrait; 12 pp.
Alaric, a film by Erin Maguire, 2004
Alaric—the interviews, a film-in-progress by Erin Maguire, 2004.
Programme to Alaric Sumner Festival (2004) A5 portrait; 8pp.
*Alaric Sumner Documentation: Documentation of his writing and other artistic
  and related output*; (2nd edn. 2004; 3rd edn. 2006) A4 portrait; 38pp.
Some initial responses, after 10 years reading, to 'Waves on Porthmeor Beach'
  by Lawrence Upton, 2005. Part 1 (Sections 1 and 2) published *Readings
  #2* and *Readings #3*.

Further source of information

Writers Forum
32 Downside Road
Sutton
Surrey
SM2 5HP

http://www.lawrenceupton.org

Elegy Walking

STEPHEN VINCENT

Walk through bereavement
Walk through, walk amongst
One ghost goes, one comes back
   A tisket, a tasket, a task:

It's odd to engage elegy as a passion and, yet, it inevitably it happens to one with the passing of a father, any family member or close friend. A passion that does not come for 'a passing moment', but enshrines itself, a quilt work of stitched moments—appearances and disappearances—as *the ghost of the absent* appoints itself a member of one's days, including, most forcefully, one's dreams at night; and then, as a presence on the street, in the countryside, or on the waters in the days and months that follow. More often than not, these are not benign appearances, but something more comparable to a dialog, an argument, or a love affair. The beloved refuses an amputation, one in which the bereaved might be allowed to quickly forget, erase everything, except for a stone monument that one erects upon a burial ground. In addition, the beloved refuses an amputation with a printed obituary, or the immediate writing of a poem, an elegy, that aspires to free one from any further intrusion by the beloved into the consciousness of our lives.

For those of us who choose to or cannot but remain open to what may be called 'the realm of the dead'—as I suggest, wittingly or not, we must—means most often finding ourselves moving into charted, difficult territory. Psychologically it is as though the earth has slipped away. We will not regain our bearings, our literal footing, this new world seems to say, until we, the bereaved, provide an answer: a calling out, a witness, an incorporation of the memory of the deceased; then a release, a grievous release from a profound, sometimes 'shrill', bondage which—though there are many return visits—slowly begins to subside. The house, the presence of the beloved is disassembled. When ideally, as though in a dream, through floor beams one sees a rich, dark earth; from which one awakes to say, now we can move on; indeed, we find ourselves with the provision, a fertile one, to do so.

After a long time, call it mourning, in contradistinction to the haunt in the popular folk song refrain, one might find oneself singing, 'She no longer walks these hills.' The long dark veil has been lifted. At this point of separation, at last, comes the full opportunity for the beloved to rise to poem, story or song. It's what some African communities are known to celebrate in what is called, a 'Second Burial.' Or, what I, a Californian, have come to call a *Walking Elegy*.

★

In my mid-twenties, I lived in Eastern Nigeria between 1965–67. A Peace Corps Volunteer, I had the good fortune to have a teaching position at the University of Nigeria, Nsukka where my classes included both 'Introduction to English Literature' and 'Creative Writing.' The East of the country was composed primarily of Igbo people and the many smaller tribes who lived amongst the creeks and bayous of the Niger delta. I knew little of Nigeria, its customs, none of its oral literature, or much of its emerging writing in English. These were still the heady days of early books of Chinua Achebe, Wole Soyinka, Christopher Okigbo and Gabriel Okara, poets and novelists. It was a ripe, deeply impressionable moment in my life—to be so young and ignorant, yet, to be in the middle of both ancient cultures combined with what became the radical growing pains of a nation beset with the multiple possibilities and dangers of modernization.

Ironically, perhaps—particularly since my ostensible role as a Volunteer from the United States role was to be identified with Nigeria's transformation into modernity—I found myself drawn to Igbo rituals that surrounded those who had died. At night, on the three days following a death—in the palm grove villages that bordered the campus—I could often hear women openly grieving, their voices variously climbing into shrieks of lament while they sat in the presence of body of the deceased. This intense expression of grief preceded the 'First Burial.' My students would tell me, particularly when a father died, the image of his passing was that of a fallen tree whose birds—the children, wives, and relatives—expressed their grief around the trunk and branches. Frequently, when I visited a student or friend's village, a wife or mother in mourning would typically cover her entire flesh in white chalk and would do so for months after the passing. At first encounter, this proximity to the death of a loved one—no matter how appropriate—was unnerving. The practice of such open grieving was entirely alien to my own family and community. Someone's death was suffered in a quiet; precious little of what was deeply felt became articulated. Young or old, the pain in one's heart was kept within in a closed and private place.

I am not a historian of death but in the context of what I know of the Protestantism in California and the West burial rituals serve as a bare, solemn cloak. The more common, and popular alternative, a Memorial Service—usually held some weeks after the death—at its best, is a genuine and moving celebration of a person's life by family, friends and figures in the local community. Yet, valuable as they are, in the process of grieving, the rituals of burial and memorial serve primarily as significant punctuation points. Neither ritual, at least to my experience, rarely goes fully to the depth of the grief, and, equally important, nor does it fully separate ones bondage to the bereaved. For the most part, the more secular the world becomes, for this experience, more often than not, we are left on our own. Which is most strange, in fact, an anathema, one suspects, to the experience of most traditional cultures. Instead of purging ones losses—no matter how either dear or historically significant—one continues to carry these ostensibly 'dead' souls inside one's being. It's an odd baggage. We might be Europeans or Euro-Americans from families who lost the majority of the children to illness from one plague or another, or those of who come from lineages that have either sponsored or been victims of Nineteenth and Twentieth century wars and acts of genocide—which include several Indian tribes here in California. We might be people coming to terms with the deaths of our immediate family members and friends. In both cases, on a collective level, wittingly or not, many of us continue to carry—as if barnacles on one's spine—the crypts of dead souls. Yet, the more 'modern' we become, one senses, we have lost the equipment to shed the dead and move forward. Perhaps not surprising, the weight and attachment to the dead makes it much harder for the bereaved to celebrate the presence of the living.

In Africa I once went for several weeks to stay with a colleague, Peter Obang, to record songs and stories in the villages of Ogoja, his home province along the Cameroon border. Often, well into the night, we recorded men and women who variously sang songs of birth, circumcision, coming-of-age, and marriage, as well as epical stories of the histories of their villages. Often we would hear powerful, funerary dirges for persons who had passed, some recent and some perhaps years ago. In the description of one evening's performance, I wrote:

> ... the man's voice emerged from a pure grief over the death of his father, "O-aye, aye, aye" he begins. The voice is first clearly focused and concentrated on celebrating the father's history. Gradually the language becomes less personal to appeal in several directions— to the people in the room, to the local gods, and to a whole history of community ancestors. A complete cosmology and code of existence is being asserted. The voice—going back to the father—rises to an insistence on the value of his position in the community and how great his loss. The song shifts to become a universal elegy, not just for this particular father, but for the death of any person who has lived fully. The voice rises to an almost shrill pitch. The singer aims his anger at the trickery, the deceitfulness of death. His eyelids stretch back as far as they can; his fingers stab the air, punctuating the song's grievous tones in what become futile gestures against death's presence. Finally, it is too much. He is overwhelmed. The trembling voice quiets. He appeals to us to be allowed to stop.

The gesture is not rhetorical. The emotion of loss is enormous; the silence in the room is almost palpable—a definite, felt sense of death's finality. It's the momentary end of the cycle before life resumes. Later I comment in my journal, "Without the language, there would be no life; without the complete cycle of songs, including epic songs of community origins and history, each had to be sung, and sung again, or chaos and dread would reign. The major responsibility falls to the singer. The physical force of the song, the weight, the tone, the power of each word makes possible both individual and communal life—while simultaneously the song holds death in vital perspective.

Looking back, in all my life, I do not believe—with a few exceptions—that I have ever been so moved, so deeply immersed and persuaded by the combination of language and song as an imaginative, authoritative and instrumental force. Performed absolutely without irony, though not lacking in breaches of humor.

*

As a University instructor of English Literature, part of the class requirement was to study 'Elegy' as one of several literary genres. Indeed, we focused on the works of Gray and Yeats, among others. Alternatively, however, I asked my students to write of the ways elegy took shape in their own villages. Indeed, it was not long before I was invited to remote villages to celebrate 'Second Burials.' In these ceremonies—six months or a year after a death—the entire community was drawn together to publicly celebrate the life of the deceased which included the history of the person's family, as well as the particular person's individual exploits and contributions to the well-being of the village. Secret societies, women's societies, the local bands, would each join to give various accounts. On a more profound level, however, the Second Burial was an occasion to acknowledge the individual's journey and struggle to prove a life worthy of entry into the local realm of the ancestors. Since death, the person's spirit was considered to have been roaming in the depths of an underworld. Tested by both evil and good ancestral spirits, the journeying also included visits back to the souls of the living. If one had committed acts of rape, murder, suicide or other grave misdeeds, the spirit was be perpetually confined to a to a limbo of wandering—in fact not even permitted a 'Second Burial.' If all was well, this final ceremony acted to elevate the spirit into the ancestral realm, a place in which the community could continue to seek counsel and profit from ancestor's particular wisdom and advice. In fact, in some villages, one could witness the carved wooden effigies of ancestral faces.

The entire day—in some places several days for major figures—would be filled with cannon volleys, drumming, music, dance and parades in which the large framed photograph of the deceased was carried under the protection of a colorfully patterned parasol. Masked and costumed members of various secret societies would dramatically enact the presence and battles with the evil spirits that still contested to possibly seize dead person's soul. Despite one's western thoughts about the empirical legitimacy of either an invisible 'underworld' or 'ancestral realm', it was impossible not to be impressed by the event's aesthetic structure. The passage between the First and the Second Burial was a dramatic and beautiful ritual through which a community could both heal itself and reassert its history and power. At 23, I was perhaps unwittingly initiated into this space but I have never forgotten the experience of the presence and struggle among powers within an invisible realm. Equally, I never imagined the way in which this experience might transmute into my own life back in the west.

*

At some point in my forties I began to walk as much as possible both alone and with friends. Alone, it was perhaps a monastic experience or, if in a group, similar to what might be called a 'peripatetic church'. In both cases the experience was a pantheistic one. On walks such gods, if we can call them that, speak from multiple sites: a voice on a cell phone in a crowd, flora & fauna, certain trees, animals, a cast of light across either a building or an open field. Temperature. To yield to a walk is to put the full field of consciousness into the play of a particular landscape. The power what I would call a 'good' walk is that moving through a particular space gives shape and resolve to one's consciousness. The outer, exterior shapes give form and strength to the interior.

From the point of view of a poet, whether or not a space discloses itself eventually as a poem—an interpretive mirroring of the walk—is never a foregone conclusion. Poet or not, sometimes the pleasure of sustained silence is juice enough. Within the walk itself, however, certain kinds of expression will often emerge. The song one starts spontaneously singing. The stones one pauses to pick and place in geometric shapes, circles, and/or towers. The stories that one makes up about the interior or external life of the perceived character of a particular shape—discovered in, say, what appears a human's shape in a rock outcropping. Thick gray fog gathered around a small, tall grove of Eucalyptus trees. A crow's shriek flight. Or, in the dark against the flashlight, the startled, amber reflection in a pair of cougar's eyes. This is to say nothing of the comparable experiences—with a very different kind of imagery—one encounters while walking in an urban space.

Indeed, if one is open—if one loosens one's illusion of containment, of innate mooring—the consciousness continuously morphs from one kind of attention into another, focusing on one shape, letting it go, dissolving into another. This ritual of what may be called 'open attention' becomes a means to find a way to cope with and shape the invisible contents of the interior life including, in the case of a death, the presence, dialog and struggle with the spirit of parted. Indeed I suspect this process is much connected to what I first appreciated in West African in the journey of the spirit between First and Second Burials. Walking—its movement, measure and pace—became a primary stake and tool in the way I would apprehend a larger, 'double' sense of the world.

*

Though elegy as a literary form may have to meet a strict set of formal requirements, there is nothing intentional about what may or may not happen during a walk. Practically, one may or may not have a simple map, a joint acceptance among friends to follow a trail from one point to another, or, alternatively nothing initially planned at all. In 'elegy walking', elegy is not an intention. It's *a fact* of a kind of consciousness. Someone is either in the process of passing—enduring long illness or decline—or is actually about to 'go over' or is 'now gone'. The 'absence' or 'presence' of whoever it is, both permeate and shape the walk: its direction, its resistances, attachment, detachment, its kinds of emotions, the register of its voice. Reciprocally, the specifics of these experiences ultimately the shape the elegy's language:

Engage the highest hill ...

Who knows the source of that command but, well served, it pulls the breath, each hard earned step, an ascent into what is actually a descent into the depths of one's consciousness and an acute heightening ones senses. Exhaustion is the way to either the grail, or, in this case, the cavity of death. The pain is sacramental. It ignites the acknowledgement, the spilling of grief. The walk gives rhythm to its song:

> Stone upon the hill.
> Stone upon the heart.
> Name upon the stone.

> Elm. Pine. Eucalyptus. Redwood.
> Dark Stone on the face.

> Knife to the bone.

> Grieving.

The walk may swing the mood in different directions. An intense anger may emerge, inevitably, as one may sense the dead, particularly 'your' dead, being publicly ignored, drifting out of community focus. The poem both cries out and questions itself amongst the anonymous, city crowd:

> Don't they know my father's dead
> And I am risen to look over the Bay
>   Over the City
> (And why would they, anyway?)

And then swings back, opening itself to the urge to crystallize, to preserve the beloved's life:

> Slants of various silvered light across the bay to the east
> Waters that he once sailed, competitively
> Boats, dark buoys and fierce youth:
> Amazing one accounts a history in one image:

183

The combination of the death and the walk is to turn one inside out; whatever the landscape—as with both Spicer and Baudelaire—the eye seeks out correspondences; the imagination draws on one, and then a succession of images. The emotion in response to the passing spirit, particularly of a person taken young—that sense of robbery—ignites the voice to enter the invisible, to contend with the figure of death himself:

> Rise Death
> Rise
> Show your face
> Let us see your hand
> Show us how you decide:
> Why you take
> When you take
> What you take
>
> Death, Death
> Rise
> Show us your bitter,
> Show us your contented face.

While part of one's consciousness contends with death, another part hears the intimations of real loss to spontaneously break into song:

> Coyote had a dog named Yukon.
>   Yukon was blind and couldn't see.
> Yukon climbed a ladder up a tree.
> A cloud picked him and took him away,
> Yipping and barking over the sea.
> Atop the mountain you can
> Hear Coyote sing, "O Yukon, Yukon
>   When will you ever ..."

Yet, once a kind of common sense begins to prevail—in acknowledgement that corporal being is gone—the walk permits an uncanny awareness and struggle with the spirit of the parted, particularly those who do not easily 'give up the ghost.'

> The dead travel with demands,
>   Not mercy. Embrace
>   Whoever—provide
>   What you can—
>   Then push them
>   Over the edge ...

Indeed the walk permits the opportunity to combat what may seem the shameless grip of the dead. To hum. To shout. To become unbearably quiet. To let the beloved appear. To cry before the appearance. To say good-bye. To let the body go overboard, to be dropped off the psyche of the bow of one's consciousness.

Sometimes that is not enough. Often the dead do not succumb so easily. One opens to another kind of dialog: how they died, where within the family or the community, what was the nature of the cause, malevolent or natural. This initial dialog or argument, one comes to realize, is not with underground spirits. To the contrary, it is an argument between the spirit of the dead, and those of us among the living. These spirits will continue to speak to one through every portal available—the wind whistling in the branches, the stranded fish on the beach, the creaking door. If the deceased were happy and productive in their life, their revisit to and hovering about the community may be similar in kind to taking a final parade in which living and dead kindly acknowledge each other. He or she may appear in the silver glow of white roses. If not, if the soul of the dead led a conflicted life, the stress, whatever the disturbance, will continue to replay itself. Such a man, so orphaned—out of terror, loss and desperation—will attempt to pull the mourner into the underworld, wanting you to be his or her escort.

The walk—and, eventually by definition, the elegy—becomes the struggle of the living not to be overtaken by the dead. One walks harder. Develops strategies:

> Engage the skulls in the neighborhood
> The one there in the black cape
> Lavender shawl, signs of a former scowl:
> Engage the skulls delicately, lick your lips
> Offer red candies, white ones, too:

Look for your brother, the one
In the fresh bones, the one
At the bottom of the stairs
The one not sure where he is:
Approach him kindly
Kiss his lips
Tug at the upper edge of his white shawl:
He's still a novice—you both are.
Offer a candy, two or three:
Give each other condolences
Awkwardly:
Drop down the walk
Away from the stairs:
Go back as one must into the world
Whatever jitters on one's lips
Or down to the base of the spine:
Grab a wet pinecone
By the trolley track:
Press its coolness to one's cheek.

Yet, there remains a price. What can one do to bestow a gift, one that
will permit the beloved the opportunity to move on. Indeed, to perform
an act, to call for a non-conditional blessing of love—the kiss—so that
the other's journey may continue. The release provides the mourner,
the walker, with 'the gift of return' to the immediate attraction and
value of life itself, the 'wet pinecone…to one's cheek.'

Yet one, in grief, will meet spirits while walking that tender the
heart and offer themselves as guides through what has been so dark:

She who lives beneath the City
Beneath the hills, she who waits, emerges
    Dissolves: She who haunts on gray days
She who lays dormant, light through fog:
She in black gown & pink sash
Who on the shoulder carries the crimson bird
    She who, she
Tells me she's mine …

Led out and Liberated from the realms of the dead, one is never that far away, the heart of the living begs some kind of connection between the two:

> ... Mountain within a mountain,
> A thick forested island
> Sometimes descends
> Down from the sky.
> Some Indians say —
> The island floated
> Over the thick gray fog—
> It is the way the dead,
> There among the trees
> Descend to announce
> A farewell, so that we
> Amongst the living
> May not suffer so much
> That they be gone.

Liberated from the underworld, one that now appears elevated, yet close, an 'elegy walk' creates its own memorials, provides characters for its shrines—in the country they are bestowed on particular rocks, within the branches of certain trees, the sounds during the year of certain streams, the odor of particular flowers. In the City, the shrines often appear spontaneously. They house grief, evoke memory, and put down a relatively solid punctuation mark on a life that has variously charmed, or even hurt us:

The Lamppost
The interior ghosted, or he who ghosted himself, the inside of his skull gone, mostly dead, the inside nocturne a series of dark memories he can no longer remember. Things knock out certain people, take out the insides of their once beautiful mercurial heads; those with the undaunted imaginations, the fearless courage; those who once climbed from valley to the highest mountain top to crow, to leap; yet, one day, something terrible crashes, something catches up, the light goes out, completely; a mystery that no one can unravel or claim; we, the lovers,

can only witness the frame, the hollow rusty metal frame, the cusp of the ceramic socket, the lamp no longer a lamp. Yet the strange red petals, the bougainvillea, slowly brocaded up, slightly aflutter around the erect pole of what barely remains of a man's body, a man's memory; the tears & sorrow steadfast for Johanna, steadfast for the disappearance—the brother, the son, the lover. The petals, the tears, the unbearably lovely tears.

Elegy Walking, finally, presents a landscape, urban or rural, which provides a scripture of communion with and separation from the beloved. Our steps and eyes provide the poem, the elegy, its shape and measure. The poem is the mirror, the re-enactment, and the ritual by which one unsheathes oneself from the embrace of the dead and opens oneself back up among the living.

Note: Poems and fragments selected from works by the author.

San Francisco, California
November 2005

Contributors' Notes

Andrea Brady teaches at Brunel University where she is co-director of the 'Archive of the Now', the university's archive of contemporary innovative writing. Her critical publications include 'Grief Work in a War Economy', *Radical Philosophy* (July/August 2002) and *English Funerary Elegy in the Seventeenth Century: Laws in Mourning* (Palgrave Macmillan, 2006). Her poetry collections include *Vacation of a Lifetime* (Salt, 2001), *Cold Calling* (Barque, 2004) and *Embrace* (Object Permanence, 2005).

Ian Davidson has contributed criticism to *Excommunicated*, a special issue of *Écorché* devoted to Paul Green, and to *Removed For Further Study: The Poetry of Tom Raworth* (The Gig, 2003), and has published *Ideas of Space in Contemporary Poetry* (Palgrave Macmillan, 2007). His poetry collections include *Harsh* (Spectacular Diseases, 2003), *Human Remains & Sudden Movements* (West House Books, 2003), *At a Stretch* (Shearsman, 2004) and *As if Only* (Shearsman, 2007).

John Hall is associate director of research and lecturer in performance writing at Dartington College of Arts. His most recent publications are *Apricot Pages* (Reality Street, 2006) and *Couldn't You?* (Shearsman, 2007).

Christine Kennedy is an artist and writer. Her publications include contributions to *In Place Of An Object* (CFAR/Aldgate Press, 2000) and *RSE 4Pack No. 4: Renga +* (Reality Street, 2002); and the collection *Possessions* (The Cherry On The Top Press, 2003). Her most recent exhibition was the group show *10x10x10* curated by UTK at Bloc Studios, Sheffield, and her most recent collection is *Nineteen Nights in San Francisco* (West House Books / The Cherry On The Top Press, 2007).

Sarah Law studied English at Cambridge and London Universities, and currently teaches Literature and Creative Writing at the University of East Anglia. She has published two collections of poetry with Stride, *Bliss Tangle* (1999) and *The Lady Chapel* (2003), and another with Shearsman Books, *Perihelion* (2006).

Peter Middleton is the author of several books including *The Male Image: Masculinity and Subjectivity in Modern Culture* (Routledge, 1992), *Distant Reading* (Alabama, 2005) and a collection of poems *Aftermath* (Salt, 2003). He teaches at the University of Southampton where he co-directs the British Electronic Poetry Centre.

Jennifer Moxley was born in 1964 and grew up in San Diego, California. Her collections include *Imagination Verses* and *The Sense Record* (both Salt, 2003) and *Often Capital* (Flood Editions, 2005). She teaches at the University of Maine.

Stuart Mugridge is an artist currently based in Birmingham. He was awarded a Year of the Artist residency in 2000 which he spent with a local conservation group and which resulted in *Sites of Cultural and Natural Interest*. A residency at Grizedale in July 2002 produced *Seven Short Walks*. For more information on his publications or practice contact him at stuartmugridge@smabs.co.uk or visit: www.smabs.co.uk

Jeremy Noel-Tod is writing a PhD at the University of Cambridge on T.S. Eliot's 'Four Quartets' and the poetry of J.H. Prynne, Geoffrey Hill and John Ashbery. He is also a freelance critic and publisher of the Landfill poetry press.

Malcolm Phillips lives and works in London. A chapbook, *Poems for my Double*, was published by Arehouse in 2005.

Peter Riley was born Stockport, Cheshire in 1940 and now lives in retirement in Cambridge. Carcanet published his selected poems, *Passing Measures*, in 2000 and the book-length poem *Alstonefield*, set in the Peak District, in 2003. Other recent publications include sketches of Transylvania collected as *The Dance at Mociu* (Shearsman, 2003), a volume of prose poems, *Excavations* (Reality Street, 2004), *A Map of Faring* (Parlor Press, 2005), *The Llyn Writings* (Shearsman, 2007) and *The Day's Final Balance: Uncollected Writings 1965-2006* (Shearsman, 2007). Critical discussions of his poetry can be found in *The Poetry of Peter Riley* (The Gig, 2000).

Michael Symmons Roberts is the author of several well-received collections, most recently *Corpus* which won the Whitbread Poetry Award for 2004. He has recently published his first novel *Patrick's Alphabet* with Cape.

Josh Robinson is a graduate student at the University of Cambridge. *Shift Report*, his first collection of poems, was published by Arehouse in 2005. His essay is adapted from a paper given at the conference on W. S. Graham in Cambridge in April 2005.

Jane Routh's *Circumnavigation* was shortlisted in 2003 for the Forward (Best First Collection) Prize. Her most recent collection, *Teach Yourself Mapmaking*, was published by Smith/Doorstop in 2006.

Penelope Shuttle has lived in Cornwall since 1970 and is the widow of the poet Peter Redgrove. Her eighth and most recent collection of poems, *Redgrove's Wife* is published by Bloodaxe Books. Her *Selected Poems* is published by Oxford Poets/Carcanet.

Zoë Skoulding's most recent collection is *The Mirror Trade* (Seren, 2004). She has a PhD in Creative and Critical Writing from the University of Wales, Bangor, where she is currently teaching in the English Department and the Department of Lifelong Learning. She co-edits *Skald* with Ian Davidson.

Lawrence Upton is a poet and an audio and graphic artist. Born in London of the Cornish diaspora, he has been based in Cornwall since 2000. He is Alaric Sumner's nominated artistic executor. Upton co-edited *Word Score Utterance Choreography* (Writers Forum, 1998) and now co-directs Writers Forum. Recent poetry includes *Wire Sculptures* (Reality Street, 2003). *Close to the literal*, co-made with composer John Levack Drever, premiered at *e-poetry 2005*.

Stephen Vincent—poet, walker, teacher, editor & publisher—lives in San Francisco. His most recent publications are the ebooks *Triggers* (www. shearsman.com) and *Sleeping With Sappho* (www.fauxpress.com). He also maintains a popular blog of commentary, poetry and photographs (http://stephenvincent.net/blog/).

Printed in the United Kingdom
by Lightning Source UK Ltd.
130330UK00001B/178/A